Body Building

Devotions to Celebrate Inclusive Community

Written by Barbara J. Newman

Library of Congress Cataloging-in-Publication Data

Newman, Barbara J., 1962-

Body Building: Devotions to Celebrate Inclusion

ISBN 978-1-936100-06-4

Bible references are taken from the New International Version, published by the Zondervan Corporation (Grand Rapids, MI).

Other titles by Barbara J. Newman:

Any Questions? A Guidebook for Inclusive Education

G.L.U.E. Training Manual

Church Welcome Story

School Welcome Story

Special Needs Smart Pages

Inclusion Awareness Lesson Kit

Inclusion Awareness Tool Kit

Autism and Your Church: Nurturing the Spiritual Growth of People with Autism Spectrum Disorders

Autism and Your Church Training DVD

The Easter Book

Helping Kids Include Kids with Disabilities

For other publications available from CLC Network
visit www.clcnetwork.org/OnlineStore

©CLC NETWORK 2009 Body Building

Pages 62-64 reproducible by purchaser only for use within an individual church, school or home and can be found online at clcnetwork.org/BodyBuilding

I dedicate this book to all of the individuals, churches, and schools who inspired these stories. May God continue to use you as teachers within the body of Christ.

Thanks also to my father, Dr. Andrew J. Bandstra, for his work as the theological editor of this book. His understanding and insights have blessed me for a lifetime, and I am deeply grateful for the commitment we share, not only as followers of Jesus Christ, but also in equipping communities to be inclusive and interdependent.

Barbara J. Newman

Preface

I finally decided to make an important change in my life. I joined a fitness center. While I have always enjoyed walking with my husband for exercise, it does little to give a workout to some sadly sagging muscle groups. The trainer patiently took me through several different machines and stations, each one of them specifically designed to work on a particular body part. While she was describing the exercises, however, she made careful note of how strengthening one area would have tremendous payoff for another area. "You can do it. One more. Working your abdomen muscles will help with your lower back." I dutifully contorted my body a few more times. "If you strengthen that portion of your leg, it might help alleviate some of the knee pain you feel at times. Keep going." As I was straining that body part one more time, it dawned on me. This fitness center is a lot like the topic of the devotion book I am writing. It's all about body building.

During my work in both schools and churches, it has been clear that each portion of the body of Christ impacts the others. If a second grade classroom includes a child with Down Syndrome, for example, each person in that classroom benefits. The children all learn from one another – each one is designed by God to bring a gift to all the others. If a church designs a worship service to include a member who has Autism, the entire church grows and learns as they worship together.

This devotion book is a celebration of God's fitness center. As we work to support and include each person, the entire body benefits and is strengthened. It is my hope and prayer that you will celebrate with me. These are lessons and stories I have accumulated during my 25 years as a special education teacher as well as a consultant to both Christian schools and churches. As you read these stories, perhaps they will help you think of your own community's fitness center. What stories do you have in your church or school that demonstrate how God uses each member of His body to impact the others?

Suggested Uses:

Christian Schools – Perhaps your school already includes children with disabilities. Perhaps you are hoping to do that in the future. It is important to remember the reasons we value an inclusive environment. God is clear in Scripture – we are to be obedient to His vision for community. As you share these devotions with students, staff, and families, it's my prayer that God will clearly reveal His picture of inclusive and interdependent community into your school.

An individual teacher may wish to read these as classroom devotions. The entire school may choose a specific week to highlight inclusion and choose one set to read during that week. The staff may wish to use this as a book study or basis for faculty devotions from time to time. The school may copy one week of this book and distribute that section to all the school's families to read at home. The school may even choose to set this book as a basis for Young Author's Month and use the challenge to write additional stories as part of the children's learning. Choose the ideas that best fit your school community.

Churches – Most churches already include some members who have disabilities. It could be an individual who had a stroke. The church may have children who have some unique learning needs. What many churches don't understand, however, is that there are most certainly people in your community who are staying home each Sunday morning because they don't know if the church would welcome them. Perhaps they have a child with Autism and were asked to leave a different church community. Perhaps there is a family member who is unable to speak and doesn't know how he would fit into the church worship setting. Statistics show that there are many, many persons with disabilities staying home on Sundays.

You may wish to use these devotions to encourage your congregation to be more welcoming. Education and information are key components in that kind of an atmosphere. As you work toward building inclusive and interdependent community, perhaps you would like to keep a copy of this book in your church library. Your children's church may want to read these as part of their setting. You may choose to have an adult small group use this as a basis for a Bible study. Your church may decide to have an inclusion awareness week where you would copy one set of these devotions to use in each home. A pastor may want to include some of the stories as part of a Sunday message. You may even want to encourage people to participate in the activity of writing and submitting a devotional from your community in response to some of the stories. Choose the ideas that best fit your church community.

Homes – These devotions are written to appeal to multi-age settings. While the stories and messages are appropriate for children, they will also speak to adults. For those families who have devotion time together, this book may serve as a helpful resource to use together. Children or adults may want to use this book, as well as the journal options, for personal devotion time. This book may also be an appropriate gift for a family member of a person with a disability. Choose the ideas the best fit your home situation.

Book Design:

The book is divided into six sections. Each portion contains seven devotions. As part of some individual readings, there are suggested activities that you could complete with a group of people. There are also suggestions for prayer. At the end of each section, there is a place for you to write your own story about someone in your home, school, or church community. We hope that many of you will choose to send those to us so that we might share these stories on our website or as part of a new devotion book produced some time in the future. (Please note: Page 64 of this book contains a form that must be filled out and signed by the highlighted individual or his/her guardian. Make a copy of the permission form or download one from the CLC Network website at www.clcnetwork/BodyBuilding. It is important to have permission before sharing information.)

If your church or school community purchased this book and would like additional copies at a discounted rate, please call CLC Network at 616.245.8388 or email glue@clcnetwork.org.

May God use these stories to spark conversations in your own community that will focus on body building.

With great anticipation for what God will do in your school, church, or home,

Barbara J. Newman

Body Building Workout: Week One

Bringing God More Clearly Into Focus Through Friendships and Interactions with People Who Have Disabilities

Does this ever happen to you? You are reading the Bible and all of a sudden you remember a person or a situation that helps you better understand that passage? I know that happens to me a lot. There are many times when I think about something that happened at school or church with a friend or student with a disability, and God uses that interaction to help me better understand a particular part of Scripture. This week of devotionals highlights some of the things I have learned about God through my friends.

Although I could write a story about each one of my students, I pray that the stories included in this workout week will serve as a springboard for you to remember the things you may have learned from people with disabilities and their friends. "Come and see what God has done, how awesome His works in man's behalf!" Psalm 66:5

Barbara J. Newman

This week's devotionals are updated from an earlier version contained in the book, *Helping Kids Include Kids with Disabilities* by Barbara J Newman (Grand Rapids, MI: Faith Alive Resources, 2001). Copyright CLC Network 2009

Body Building

Day 1
Image-bearers of God

Bible Reading: Genesis 1:24-31
Key Verse: "So God created man in His own image, in the image of God He created him; male and female He created them." Genesis 1:27

Devotional: How many things do you have in your home that were not there 30 years ago? Look around you. Do you have a computer with access to the Internet? What about a cell phone? How many of you had a DVD player 30 years ago? Do you have remote controls for your various electronic gadgets? How about Louise? Louise? Yes, she would not have been in your home 30 years ago either.

Louise is a 60-year-old woman who is cognitively impaired. Thirty years ago, Louise lived in an institution. At that time, Louise would not have been welcome in our homes or communities. That's why she lived in a building with other people, all of whom had cognitive impairments. Unfortunately, the people who operated this building did not understand our Bible verse for today; they didn't realize that Louise was made in God's image. If they had understood this, Louise would still have some hair.

When I met Louise, she no longer had any hair on her body. Even the fine hair on her arms and legs was gone. When Louise was at the institution, she was used in an experiment. Doctors gave her medicine that they eventually wanted to give to cancer patients. Even though Louise did not have cancer, they wanted to see what the effects would be when someone took this drug. The doctors discovered that this cancer medication caused all of a person's hair to fall out and stay out.

Louise moved out of that institution about 30 years ago, and she is now enjoying life in a small group home with good caretakers who understand that she is an image-bearer of God. She can enjoy her own living room and kitchen in place of the large hall at the institution where all of the residents had to eat together. One of her favorite places now is the bedroom she shares with only one other person, instead of a giant room where all the people had to sleep on unkempt and smelly bedding.

Although Louise is now enjoying the dignity she deserves as an image-bearer of God, her hair will never grow back. Forgive us, God, for not seeing your image in Louise. And Louise, on behalf of us all, please accept our apology. Even though you have been unable to speak, and therefore have not used your mouth to confess Jesus as your Savior, your actions have reflected the same love and care for your abusers that Jesus showed for His. God has used your life as an example of who Jesus is.

Prayer: Lord, forgive us when we fail to see your image in those around us. Give us your eyes as we look at the precious and holy people who surround our lives. Thank you also for treasuring us. In Jesus' name, amen.

WEEK ONE

Day 2
Modern-day Miracles

Bible Reading: John 2:1-11
Key Verse: "This, the first of his miraculous signs, Jesus performed at Cana in Galilee. He thus revealed His glory, and His disciples put their faith in Him." John 2:11

Devotional: Do you believe in miracles? I remember the joy of holding my two sons in my arms after giving birth to them. I counted their small, slender fingers, checked their tiny ears to see if they worked, marveled at the delicate toenails, and put up a fuss when the nurse had to return them to the hospital nursery. The miracle of birth happens often, and it is wondrous each and every time.

I remember, however, hearing about one mother's experience that was very different from mine. After her little girl was born, she was not allowed to hold her. Instead, this little girl was rushed by helicopter to another hospital with more advanced facilities. The doctor called the mother who had just given birth, saying, "Your baby probably won't survive this trip." This baby's mother and father had no idea whether they had given birth to a boy or girl, or whether they would ever hold that child alive. Do you believe in miracles?

The parents found out the next morning that their baby was a girl, and that she was still alive, although the doctors did not expect her to live very long. Through a grueling three years of hospital visits, resuscitations, prayers, daily doctor calls, and various medical procedures, their daughter continued to live. During each crisis, the doctors would say, "We don't expect your daughter to make it," or "Your child will never talk, eat, or walk." Well, this child, along with her siblings, was a student at our Christian school. She could eat and run, and sometimes we had to tell her to be quiet because she was talking too much. Do you believe in miracles?

Jesus performed many miracles that are recorded in the Bible. Each time I read about them, I am amazed. While I was growing up I thought that miracles were reserved for Biblical times. I never expected to witness miracles during my lifetime. Thanks to the students in my life, I now believe that God is just as willing and able to do miracles today as He was in Biblical times. Many of the students in our inclusive education program are truly living miracles. Some of you may be familiar with such miracle children in your own church or school. Each time I see one of these children, my faith in our powerful God is strengthened. Out of His amazing love for us, God continues to reach into our hopeless situations and change the course of nature. Do you believe in miracles? Spend some time with such children and you will.

Prayer: Our loving Father in heaven, we thank you for reaching into our lives in large and small ways. We thank you for our salvation, the miracle you make available to each one of us. We praise you for the many walking miracles in our time that remind us of your power and love. In Jesus' name, amen.

Body Building

Day 3
A Sweet Sound to God

Bible Reading: I Samuel 16:1-13

Key Verse: "But the Lord said to Samuel, 'Do not consider his appearance or his height, for I have rejected him. The Lord does not look at the things man looks at. Man looks at the outward appearance, but the Lord looks at the heart." I Samuel 16:7

Devotional: For many years, I had the privilege of directing the CLC Choir, a group of 30 students who have disabilities. This group of children and adults touched the hearts of many people in the West Michigan area by singing in churches and visually demonstrating the spectrum of people God includes in His family.

For a number of years, I had the pleasure of singing in the Calvin College Alumni Choir. This group also frequented churches in the West Michigan area, inspiring people with the excellence and beauty of their harmonies and the precisely delivered musical texts from inspired composers.

One week, the Alumni Choir sang at a church in Grand Rapids, and by coincidence, it was followed the next week by the CLC choir. As the CLC choir was practicing, I thought about the beautiful harmonies of the previous week and felt a bit awkward about the four numbers we would sing, quite monotone and disjointed in comparison. As I watched the faces of the choir members, though, God allowed me a glimpse from His point of view.

From a purely musical standpoint, these two choirs could not be compared, and it seemed we had no business even performing from the same choir loft. From God's perspective, however, these students were praising Him from their hearts. The joy on their faces and the enthusiasm for Jesus they so clearly presented combined to make an angelic chorus for God. The songs they sang were as pure to God as the state of their hearts.

I could only hope that I had portrayed the same sincere joy and gratitude to God as I sang with the Alumni Choir the week before. I was reminded that God looks at the state of our hearts as He accepts our efforts. Our work means nothing if it is not offered with a pure heart. The students in this choir taught me an important lesson, one that I continue to learn anew each day. Even as we are tempted to evaluate people and events by human standards, God will continue to measure our offerings by looking at our hearts.

Prayer: Dear Lord, we confess that our hearts are not always filled with pure motives. We admit our pride and dishonesty. We ask that you replace our sinfulness with your purity and holiness. May our lives be sweet music to your ears as you examine and change our hearts. In Jesus' name, amen.

WEEK ONE

Day 4
"Yeah, God!"

Bible Reading: Matthew 18:1-6

Key Verse: "He called a little child and had him stand among them. And He said: 'I tell you the truth, unless you change and become like little children, you will never enter the kingdom of heaven.'" Matthew 18:2-3

Devotional: Admittedly, I am no great basketball fan. I did, however, enjoy attending a recent high school game. I was amazed at the enthusiasm of the fans as they rose to their feet, cheering for their talented team. You should have heard the cheers and noise of the crowd as their team kept sinking basket after basket.

Have you ever experienced the same enthusiasm and excitement in church? When was the last time we jumped up and yelled our praise to God because someone became a Christian? Even the excitement of winning a basketball game with a buzzer-beating three-point shot cannot compare to the happiness we should feel when see someone give his or her life to Jesus. So why is it so easy for us to jump and yell at a basketball game when we have such a difficult time giving expression to these feelings for God?

It was close to Easter in my classroom, and we had been discussing the "sad day" and the "happy day" all week. As we were reviewing the story one last time, I asked a student to tell us about the sad day. Although speaking is difficult for him, he answered, "Jesus die." He has a beautiful love for Jesus, and his face showed some of the pain and sadness Jesus must have felt. When I asked him to tell me about the happy day, he jumped out of his chair, started hugging the other children, and hopped up and down, saying, "Jesus alive!"

As I remember this moving moment, I try to emulate the joy this student expressed about the miracle of salvation. With full freedom from social constraint, he was able to tell others and God about his love for Jesus. In the midst of our "proper" lives, may we challenge ourselves to express a childlike faith. May our love and enthusiasm for Jesus be contagious as we ask Him to shine through us. We would have nothing without God, but with salvation in Jesus, the forces of evil never make the winning shot. God does. "Yeah, God!"

Prayer: Dear Father in heaven, our hearts are overflowing with praise for you. May your Spirit rule in our lives so that we will give daily expression to our love for you. In Jesus' name, amen.

Body Building

Day 5
What's So Special About This Christian School?

Bible Reading: Genesis 12:1-5

Key Verse: "The Lord had said to Abram, 'Leave your country, your people and your father's household and go to the land I will show you.'" Genesis 12:1

Devotional: The author of Hebrews recounts this remarkable move by saying, "By faith Abraham, when called to go to a place he would later receive as his inheritance, obeyed and went, even though he did not know where he was going" (Hebrews 11:8). The writer of Hebrews goes on to explain that Abraham trusted God with everything he had.

Can you imagine leaving everything you have in order to settle in a new place? You would have to say goodbye to your family, friends, house, and possessions. Indeed, you would have to leave your whole community behind. Why would Abraham do such a thing? It must have taken a lot of trust to know that God had something truly wonderful in store for him.

I had the privilege of meeting a modern-day Abraham and Sarah. They moved across the country, leaving home, church, friends, and city behind in order to follow God's call for one of their children. They moved to our community so that their daughter who has Autism could attend a Christian school. After doing a thorough search, they discovered that Christian special education is a rare commodity in our country. Some of the children in the public schools in their former community had taught their child that "Christians have cooties," and that "You shouldn't play with Christians." Knowing that their daughter's eternal salvation is more important than all earthly possessions, this family has joined our community so that their child can be surrounded and supported by peers and teachers who love Jesus.

This kind of Christian schooling should be available to all students with disabilities. We should be able to surround all such students with God's love in welcoming them to our Christian schools and church communities. All children with disabilities should have the opportunity to grow to love Jesus in an educational environment that values them as an important part of God's family.

Prayer: We thank you, Father, for Christian special education. We pray for the many children who do not have this service in their own communities. Work in the hearts of Christian people so that they will enfold children with disabilities into Christian schools in their own areas. In Jesus' name, amen.

WEEK ONE

Day 6
The Untouchables

Bible Reading: Matthew 8:1-4

Key Verses: "A man with leprosy came and knelt before Him and said, 'Lord, if you are willing, you can make me clean.' Jesus reached out His hand and touched the man. 'I am willing,' He said. 'Be clean!' Immediately he was cured of his leprosy." Matthew 8:2-3

Devotional: Can you think of anything so gross that it makes you feel sick? I'll spare you the details, but I remember someone throwing up all over his mom after eating Thanksgiving dinner. That was disgusting. I also get a sick feeling when I think about touching a snake. Yuck!

I'm not sure, but I would imagine that people during Biblical times felt the same way about touching people who had leprosy. They felt it was disgusting to touch someone who had sores on his or her body or perhaps was missing body parts. Declared to be unclean, people with leprosy were confined to leper colonies, isolated from everyone else.

One day, a man escaped from one of these leper colonies and found Jesus, having heard of His power to heal. The people probably cleared right out of his way as he came to ask Jesus to help him. Then Jesus did something amazing: Jesus touched this man, a man who probably had not been touched by anyone in years. And then He did something even more remarkable: Jesus healed the man of his leprosy.

Although we no longer have leper colonies, we sometimes isolate people based on their appearance or condition. Have you ever been at the mall and met someone with a disability? Perhaps the person had a face that was disfigured or a body that needed a wheelchair. Maybe you weren't sure what to do, and so in some way you showed that you felt this person was "unclean." This sort of experience can leave us feeling uncomfortable.

I will never forget a young student of mine who had a severe drooling problem. Although this deterred me from touching his hands, some of his friends reminded me of the healing touch of Jesus. Never put out by the wet and slimy hands, this student's two faithful friends would hold his hands and help him out to the playground. They would grab his slimy coat and zip it up for him. These friends never showed anxiety about touching him. I would think, "What if the saliva passes germs," not remembering that when we do the work of Jesus, He will protect us.

I want to thank these two friends who said, "I am willing." They remind me of the power of touch as we minister in the name of Jesus. They communicated unconditional love and acceptance to a child who had previously been considered "unclean." May God bless them and the many other children who have used the healing power of Jesus to touch the lives of those with disabilities. They have taught me much.

Prayer: Lord, help us to touch others in your name. We want to be your servants. In Jesus' name, amen.

Body Building

Day 7
Andrea, John, Lana, and Theresa

Bible Reading: Revelation 21:1-4

Key Verse: "He will wipe every tear from their eyes. There will be no more death or mourning or crying or pain, for the old order of things has passed away." Revelation 21:4

Devotional: Andrea was a wonderful child. She had difficulty speaking due to her larger tongue and small mouth cavity that often characterizes people with Down syndrome. Andrea's spark and joy in life were contagious, however, and she loved singing time, often requesting her favorites.

One day, Andrea was trying to tell us her song request. To make herself clear, she pointed vigorously to her shoes and then to her tongue. The sign language helped us understand that she wanted the song, "Have you got feet, and can you walk? Have you got a tongue, and can you talk? Oh, yes. Oh, yes. Then you've got something to thank God for." We sang that song together.

Later that day, in the evening, Andrea became very ill. For some unknown reason, her lungs filled up with fluid and she died. It was quite a shock to our school community. We cried through her funeral right along with the family. While the minister was speaking, I remembered Andrea's song request. Although it did not take away the pain of a young life lost, we knew that Andrea could no longer be hindered in her praise to God by her tongue, her mouth, or her Down Syndrome. She had everything to thank God for. The praise time in our room paled in comparison to the choir she would join in heaven.

There have been four times during my years as a teacher that we have experienced the death of one of our students. I have been blessed personally by each one of these children fashioned in the image of God. Each child has made a contribution to the body of Christ, and I am grateful to have learned from them.

Although I miss these dear ones, they have given me a chance to picture our heavenly home. And as I picture this home, I see the entire Christian community transported to a place where we can truly and fully function as the body of Christ. Unencumbered by the constraints of this world, we will join Andrea, John, Lana, and Theresa in living for eternity in the presence of God. They have preceded us to a place where there is no more death or mourning or crying or pain. In the meantime, may we enjoy the community of believers as we experience it together, learning from every one and valuing each person as a member of Christ's body.

Prayer: Lord God, we thank you for calling us to spend eternity with you. We also thank you for allowing us to experience your presence by communing with the body of Christ here on earth. May your love flow to us and through us as we live together. In Jesus' name, amen.

WEEK ONE

A Story of Your Own

As you think about the people in your life who may have a disability, perhaps you remember something that interaction or friendship has taught you about God. Use this page to tell a story of your own. Remember, if you would like to do so, follow the instructions in the back of this book and send it to us. We want to learn from your stories, too.

Bible Reading:

Key Verse:

Devotional:

Activity:

Prayer:

Body Building Workout: Week Two

Learning from God's Stories and Church Stories

I grew up in the inner city of Grand Rapids. While I appreciated the stars at night, the city is always light. The street lights shine through the window shades and in your face while you are trying to sleep. Businesses and some houses have lights that are always brightly burning. When I looked up at the stars at night, I could only view them through the night lights.

On some summer weekends, our family would go camping. We would leave those city lights and trade them in for campfire light. When darkness would fall, I would look up and see the beautiful stars and night sky. It was brilliant. As a family we would comment to each other, "I have never seen the stars quite like this before."

Sometimes it takes a new setting or situation so that you can see something more clearly or in a different way. I am so thankful for many of my friends with disabilities, as well as their churches. This set of stories allows me to see some things differently. As I look at church celebrations such as salvation, new members' class, baptism, profession of faith, and ministering to others through the stories in this section, I can truly say, "I have never seen these events quite like this before." It is my prayer that you will say the same thing after reading these devotionals.

Barbara J. Newman

Copyright CLC Network 2009.

WEEK TWO

Day 1
Salvation and My Friend Jessica

Bible Reading: II Corinthians 3:12-18
Key Verses: "And we, who with unveiled faces all reflect the Lord's glory, are being transformed into His likeness with ever-increasing glory, which comes from the Lord, who is the Spirit." II Corinthians 3:17-18

Devotional: My friend in Wisconsin has a very special outfit. He is a beekeeper. In addition to wearing long sleeves, pants, and special gloves, there is a hat that includes a net for covering his face. Whenever he works with the hives, he makes sure that face covering is in place. Beekeepers and brides often wear a veil to cover the face.

Sometimes I think Christians wear a veil, too. We might be talking or singing about the most amazing truth about Jesus, and sometimes we don't even smile or show excitement on our faces. It's like we are wearing a veil to cover up what Jesus has done. That's the reason why Jessica changed my life. She is a friend without a veil.

I have had the joy of witnessing several people give their lives to Jesus. That person goes from being dead, destined to live eternity separated from God, sick with sin and infected with the power of Satan to being free in Jesus Christ. This person is now a forgiven, dearly loved, and eternally secure saint who is free from the power of the evil one. It's the most opposite and amazing transformation one could ever make.

One of these transformations, however, was the most dramatic I have ever witnessed. My friend Jessica wanted nothing to do with Jesus. In fact, she would get upset and growl any time people mentioned His name. Jessica happens to have Autism, and so while another person might cover up these feelings, Jessica didn't understand how to do that. She was very honest about her fear and dislike. But I had the joy of being with her when she gave her life to Jesus. As she prayed to ask Jesus into her life, I was able to witness the power of the gift of salvation. You see, Jessica never wears a veil over her face. When the Bible talks about having an "unveiled face" that can reflect the Lord's glory, I think of what I witnessed that day. Jessica knew very little about being a Christian, but in that moment I was able to see a total transformation through the power of the Holy Spirit. She went from growling about Jesus to telling everyone about Jesus. She went from having a scowling, angry face to having an inner joy that poured out of her. Jessica switched from one who wanted nothing to do with God to a person who couldn't ask enough questions about her new faith in Jesus. This did not take days or even hours to happen. It was immediate. She continues to reflect the Lord's glory.

Jessica's unveiled face is a great reminder to me. I want to reflect the changes that God has made in my life to others. I want people to see, just like the Israelites saw on the face of Moses, that I get to live my life in God's presence.

Body Building

Activity: Talk about it. Do you ever wear a veil over your Christian life? Can people tell that God has transformed you into a new creation? Are there changes you want to make?

Prayer: Thank God for the transformation He has made in your life. Ask Him to let your light shine to others.

Day 2
New Members' Class

Bible Reading: I Corinthians 12: 21-26

Key Verse: "If one part suffers, every part suffers with it; if one part is honored, every part rejoices with it." I Corinthians 12:26

Devotional: While I would never want to be on a sled for 1150 miles in temperatures well below zero with only my dogs for companionship, I certainly enjoyed watching a TV special about the Iditarod. This Alaskan race takes great courage and teamwork. The dogs are carefully arranged and tied together as they make their way through treacherous terrain. The musher knows just how to arrange them and care for them as they race towards the finish line.

    I visited a United Methodist church that reminded me a lot of these dog sled units. They figured out how important it is to all pull together. There were several people ready to make a commitment and join this church. They spent time learning about the church in something they call the "New Members' Class." Two members of this group were in wheelchairs. Sunday arrived and the class was to go up on the stage to be introduced to the congregation and welcomed into that fellowship. While 14 of the group members could have used the steps to the stage, two members would need to approach the stage from the side and up the ramp. This perceptive group realized that they were all tied together. Instead of separating, all 16 new members came on the stage up the ramp, showing their unity. They were all moving together – in the words of the Three Musketeers, "All for one, and one for all."

    Our key verse for today is another way of talking about the New Member's Class and the church. The Bible tells us that we are all tied together. If one person in the church is hurting, we all hurt. If one person in the church is rejoicing, we all rejoice. Just like the sled dogs all have a different and important position on the rope, each of us has a unique and vital position in the body of Christ. When one of the dogs slows down or needs a rest, the whole team adjusts to the needs of that member of the team. When one of the dogs catches a gust of energy, it can pull the whole team along. That's how we are tied together with one another.

    May that set of new members from the United Methodist Church inspire the congregation with their attitude and spread it to all the members. As they join that church team, may the whole group realize that they are "All for one, and one for all."

Activity: Gather a photograph from each member of your small group. If you were to arrange your group into a pulling team, how would it be arranged? Don't forget to put in the picture of the team musher! Where does Jesus stand?

Prayer: As a group, lift up someone who may be hurting. Then rejoice with someone who is rejoicing. Offer these prayers of petition and praise.

Body Building

Day 3
Welcome to the Family and the Baby Paul

Bible Reading: Matthew 18:1-6
Key Verse: "…and whoever welcomes a little child like this in my name, welcomes me." Matthew 18:5

Devotional: When a baby is almost ready to be born, there are many preparations a family makes. They often prepare a special room where the baby will sleep. They need to stock up on things like diapers, baby blankets, a tiny bathtub, children's books, and much more. The parents are getting ready to welcome a new child into their family.

A church is like a family, too. Most churches have a way to welcome a new baby into the church family. Some will hold a celebration called baby dedication. Other churches practice infant baptism. While these are different celebrations, they both make one very clear statement to the little child: "Welcome to the Family."

Several years ago, my friends were getting ready for their new baby. They didn't know if God would send them a baby girl or boy. They didn't know what color hair the baby would have or what their child would love to do later in life. My friends did know, however, that God was the one in charge. He was mixing together a recipe for a very special and treasured person. This child was a gift God was giving to their family and their church family. When the little boy was born, they knew a lot more about his God recipe. Not only was he a boy who would grow up to love music, people, and God very much, he also happened to have something called Down Syndrome. Where most people have 46 of the chromosomes that God uses as building blocks for His "people recipe," Paul has 47.

When the day came for Paul to be baptized, his parents asked me to help sing a song to him – a song that would make sure Paul's family and the others in the church knew that this little child was an honored and welcomed member of God's family. "Welcome to the family. We're glad that you have come to share your life with us, as we grow in love. And may we always be to you what God would have us be – a family always there – to be strong and to lean on" ("Welcome to the Family" by Natalie Sleeth).

Another family had a child who was born with Down Syndrome. As their priest was helping them prepare for the special day, the baby's father said to him, "Don't baptize her unless you are ready to include her." That child's dad wanted to make sure the church was really welcoming her, not just for one day, but for her whole life. I am guessing that the priest heard the voice of Jesus saying, "And whoever welcomes a little child like this in my name, welcomes me." (Matthew 18:5)

Activity: Whether it's a new baby or a new Christian, it is important to God that we welcome people into His family. What are some ways you can help do this?

Prayer: Thank God for the newest member of your church or small group. Ask Him to help you be good at welcoming others.

Day 4
Marie's Way of Speaking

Bible Reading: Romans 10:5-13
Key Verse: "If you confess with your mouth, 'Jesus is Lord,' and believe in your heart that God raised Him from the dead, you will be saved." Romans 10:9

Devotional: Just as churches have different ways of saying to a baby, "Welcome to the family," churches also give believers in Jesus different ways of telling others that they want to follow Him. Some churches have infant baptism and then encourage people to make profession of faith when they get old enough to stand up and tell others that they love Jesus. Other churches might have a baby dedication and then use baptism when the person is older and able to tell people that he or she has chosen to follow Jesus. Whatever practice your church has, it's important to make a statement that you are following Jesus. Our verse today tells us that when we tell other people that Jesus is the Lord of our life, and we believe that He is alive today, we will be saved.

My friend Marie loves Jesus. Not only is she faithful in attending church, she also helps others at church by praying for them during the week. Marie never says these prayers out loud, only in her heart and mind. Marie can't speak with her mouth, but she has many ways she can communicate.

Marie is in a wheelchair. It's hard for her to control most of the parts of her body. Even if she wanted to pick up her arm or move one of her fingers, she couldn't do that. She can, however, control her eyes. If you ask her a question and the answer is "yes," she will look at you. If the answer is "no," she will look away. She has a chart with words on it. People who spend time with Marie know how to run their fingers over the words and watch her eyes to know what she wants to say. On a very special Easter Sunday, we all knew what Marie wanted to say. She wanted to tell everyone that she is a follower of Jesus. She asked to be baptized.

This church has a small pool that people climb in when they are baptized. The pastor dips them under the water as a way to show that their sins are washed away because Jesus died and rose again. How would Marie get in the pool? Could she be baptized, too? Marie's friends gathered around her wheelchair that day. They lifted Marie's body into the small pool and helped the pastor as he baptized Marie.

Marie helped people that day. She helped everyone remember that whether you say words with your mouth or whether you use your eyes to pick out the words you want to say, it is very important to tell people what is in your heart. Let other people know that you want to follow Jesus.

Activity: There are many ways you can tell other people about your love for Jesus. Name some of them. What is something you could do today to let people know?

Prayer: While it's important to tell others you love Jesus, it's even more important to let Jesus know you love Him. Use your prayer time today to communicate that clearly.

Body Building

Day 5
Caught on Film

Bible Reading: I Timothy 4:9-14

Key Verse: "Don't let anyone look down on you because you are young, but set an example for the believers in speech, in life, in love, in faith and in purity." I Timothy 9:12

Devotional: We had a long trip to Iowa ahead of us. My sister Ruth and I were in the back seat of the car. She is very good at knitting and crocheting, and I wanted to learn. I picked out this wonderful multi-colored yarn, and she patiently showed me how to move the crochet hook to chain that yarn in place. When I got stuck, Ruth would take her own crochet hook and show me what to do next on her project so that I could learn what to do with my yarn and hook. Time after time, she was my example of how to crochet.

Examples are very important. Sometimes when I would get stuck on a math problem, I would study the example to see if it would show me how to get "unstuck." When I needed to arrange pictures in a scrapbook, I used the Internet to study samples that other people had put together. Our verse today talks about how important examples are to Christians. Sometimes we can look at others to help us figure out how to speak, live, love, show faith, and show purity.

One church had six young people who wanted to make profession of faith. These individuals were all teenagers. Instead of having each person stand up on a Sunday morning and talk in front of the whole group, the church wanted to show more about how these young people lived out their faith in Jesus. So, a person from the congregation used a video camera to capture answers to questions and show a little bit about each person's life outside of church. As I watched each young person tell and show their commitment to Christ, I was reminded of the verse for today. The video showed young people who were setting an example for others – showing us good ways to talk and live.

One of the people on the video, however, caught my attention in a special way. It was harder to understand her words, but she was very excited about Jesus and the church. When asked what was so special about her church, she said that everyone knew her name. What a great goal for churches – to know the name of each teenager. When asked about Jesus, she said, "I love Jesus." Her answers were not long, but each one was given with great excitement from her heart. I wanted to remember her as an example to myself. Big words and long answers don't mean anything unless they come with joy from the heart. While this young woman may struggle to read, speak, and learn, God used her as an example to me – she set an example for me in speech, life, love, faith, and purity. Thank you, God, for catching that on film!

Activity: Think about the people in your life. Can you think of some people who set an example for you in how to live as a Christian? Share these names.

Prayer: Thank God for these examples of Christian living.

WEEK TWO

Day 6
A Story with a Sad Ending

Bible Reading: I Peter 2:13-17
Key Verse: "Show proper respect to everyone: Love the brotherhood of believers, fear God, honor the king." I Peter 2:17

Devotional: Not all stories have happy endings. Sometimes the puppy dies, the dad moves away, the mom gets sick, or the child loses an important keepsake. This is one of those stories. It doesn't have a happy ending – at least not yet. I am telling this story, however, because sometimes we can learn from the situations of others. Don't let this happen to you!

There was a young man who was baptized as an infant and was now ready to tell other people that he was a follower of Jesus. He wanted to make profession of faith and join the church. He wanted to take communion with the others in his church community. This person knew how important the church is, and he went faithfully on Sundays, but he also left immediately after the church service was over. He would come to the worship service and taste all of the good things that God wanted to give him, but that sweet taste would turn very sour as he looked around at the others in his church. There was no way he could stand and look at some of those people and join the church.

This young man had been part of the same church community all of his life. He went to Sunday School and then to youth group. While he was growing up, his parents and teachers thought that there might be some differences in the way he was developing. He did great in school academically, but it was hard for him to always know what to say to friends. Also, he loved his video games so much, it was hard for him to think about other things at times. The doctors finally decided he has something called Asperger Syndrome. His friends at church, however, didn't seem to know or care much about that. They could be very cruel to him – calling him names and teasing him. They would make jokes about him to others and let him know that they did not want him around. This young man finally stopped attending youth group, because the other young people were so unkind. As he thought of standing up in front of his congregation and telling people about his love for Jesus, he also thought of looking at their faces. He decided not to join the church, and he decided to stay home on Sundays and play video games instead. It was safer at home than at church.

I'm not sure if this person will ever be able to break off a piece of bread and dip it in the cup and remember the sacrifice of Jesus and His body. I'm not sure about that because the church – that body of Christ – did not understand how very important it is to treat each person with honor and respect. God is very clear about this, and yet, this church didn't practice what God was showing them.

Don't let this happen in your community. Make sure you welcome each person and treat one another with the honor and respect God expects of us.

Body Building

Activity: Write this church a letter. What advice would you give them in how to treat one another?

Prayer: Pray for this young man. I can't tell you his name, but there are more people just like him. Pray that God would give him the strength to go back through the doors of the church and surround him with people who can respect him and honor him for the gifts he has to share with them.

WEEK TWO

Day 7
May I Help You?

Bible Reading: II Corinthians 9:6-15
Key Verse: "This service that you perform is not only supplying the needs of God's people but is also overflowing in many expressions of thanks to God." II Corinthians 9:12

Devotional: The family entered the church. They had so many things on their minds! While they were very excited about the new baby that was coming very soon, the doctors had done some tests on the baby before it was even born. They found out that the baby, a little boy, had Down Syndrome. These parents didn't know what that would mean for this child or for their family. Would this little one ever be able to say "mom" and "dad?" Would this baby ever grow up to love pizza and go out to movies? Would he be able to play t-ball or soccer with other children from the neighborhood? Would he drive a car or get married some day? They had so many questions, and one of the most important questions they had was about God. Would their little boy ever know Jesus? Would he be able to pray and sing? They didn't always go to church, but they did today. These parents wanted to ask God to show them more about this new baby who would be born very soon. God is amazing. He knew their thoughts and big questions. He had already prepared an answer.

The church they picked at random that morning was certainly not at random for God. You see, this church understood very clearly that each person is to be honored and that God has gifted each individual to fill a spot in His kingdom. One young man in this church serves as a greeter. He also comes in on Fridays to be part of the men's Bible study and also stays around to help clean the floors of the worship center. He is active in both giving and receiving. He is a hard worker, very friendly, and he also happens to have Down Syndrome. Imagine the surprise that awaited the visiting family. The first person to greet them in this church was a very friendly young man who shook their hands, identified them as visitors, welcomed them and introduced them to others, and also happened to have Down Syndrome. They started to cry as they clearly understood that God had heard all of their questions and provided His direct answers in the form of a young man who was placed by God in that spot at that time.

So often we look at individuals with disabilities as people we need to serve. This church understood, however, that this young man has been called by God to serve others. God used him in a powerful way that day.

Activity: In what ways has God gifted you? Talk about how He can use that gift to help and serve others.

Prayer: Ask God for opportunities today to use your gifts to serve others. Who knows what ways God will use you to touch the life of someone else.

Body Building

A Story of Your Own

Use this page to tell a story of your own. Is there a person in your life with a disability who has helped you see something in a new way? Tell that story here. Remember, if you would like to do so, follow the instructions in the back of this book and send it to us. We want to learn from your stories, too.

Bible Reading:

Key Verse:

Devotional:

Activity:

Prayer:

WEEK THREE

Body Building Workout:
Week Three

Learning from God's Stories and School Stories

Each morning as I drive to school, I give thanks for the inclusive education programs in the CLC Network partner schools where I teach and consult. Examples of love and belonging abound each day in these schools, where I see children with and without disabilities living out the model for the church the apostle Paul described in I Corinthians 12. We are one body together in Christ. At these schools, God is using students with disabilities to teach many things to everyone around them, and the lessons are a two-way street. The children enrich my life and teach me so many things that at the end of my day I often wonder who has been the teacher and who the student.

This should not surprise us. In these seven devotions, I will provide you with some Biblical examples of God's emphasis on people with disabilities, and on the gifts they have to offer the Christian community. My prayer is that this week of reading and meditation will allow us all to see how special the Christian community is and how God has honored us with the presence of people with disabilities.

Barbara J. Newman

This week's devotionals are updated from an earlier version contained in the book, *Helping Kids Include Kids with Disabilities* by Barbara J Newman (Grand Rapids, MI: Faith Alive Resources, 2001). Copyright CLC Network 2009.

27

Body Building

Day 1
God's Knitting Pattern

Bible Reading: Psalm 139:1-16

Key Verses: "For you created my inmost being; you knit me together in my mother's womb. I praise you because I am fearfully and wonderfully made; your works are wonderful, I know that full well." Psalm 139:13-14

Devotional: Did you know that God can knit? I never learned how to knit, but my mother did. She could make soft white baby blankets, colorful large afghans, warm winter sweaters, and mittens for snowy days. On Christmas Eve one year, I remember opening a package of hand-knit clothes for my Barbie doll.

In Psalm 139:13, the Bible tells us that God knits. Do you think He knits sweaters or Barbie doll clothes? No. He knits people. Just like my mom used a special pattern for her hand-knit items, God has a special pattern He used to make you. What color eyes, skin, and hair do you have? Look at your fingerprints. Did you know that no one else in the whole world has fingerprints that match the ones on your hands?

The writer of Psalm 139 tells us that God is the one who planned and decided everything about us before we were even born. He watched you while you were developing inside your mother, and He wove together the person you would become. He decided the right combination for you, and made you according to His perfect plan. Each one of God's children is very special.

God has a reason for making each of us the way we are. He has a job for you, and only you will be able to do that job. If you are a fast runner, God wants you to use that talent for Him. If you are an excellent reader, God wants you to use that gift for Him. Perhaps you were born with some kind of a disability. God has a special plan for you and gifts you can offer Him. God made no mistakes while knitting us together. He planned and created us exactly the way He wants us to be.

This week as we look at a variety of Bible stories that deal with people with disabilities, you will see the incredible gifts that each person has to offer. Each one is a blessing from God to His people. In fact, you will see that people with disabilities are necessary to our churches and communities. By excluding even one person, the faith life of God's people would be severely lacking. Let us praise God that each one of us is "fearfully and wonderfully made."

Activity: Gather your family or group members in a circle. Take time to talk together. What is unique about each person? What knitting pattern did God use to make that person? Talk about what God's plan may be for each one.

Prayer: Offer a prayer of thanksgiving for who you are. Thank God that He is the perfect weaver. Thank God for your family or group members and their special qualities.

Day 2
Awesome God

Bible Reading: John 9:1-12, 35-41

Key Verse: "'Neither this man nor his parents sinned,' said Jesus, 'but this happened so that the work of God might be displayed in his life.'" John 9:3

Devotional: Have you ever taken a trip to the mountains? The first time you saw a mountain, what did you think? When I first drove toward the Rocky Mountains, I was shocked. They are huge, majestic, powerful, beautiful, and each mountain was made by God. Mountains testify to the fact that we serve an awesome and powerful God.

God uses many ways to show us His power. One way He chooses to let us know He is working in our world is through the lives of people with disabilities. Having a disability used to be understood as a sign that either those who have them or their parents must have done something especially sinful. In John 9, however, Jesus tells us that this is not true. People with disabilities have an important message to tell us through their lives: namely, that God is working in our world.

When Jaden was born, she was very sick. Her parents were not even sure that Jaden would live. The doctor took her parents into a special room and gave his predictions. If Jaden lived, the doctor said she would never be able to run. He also said that Jaden would never dance.

But God had a different plan for Jaden. He worked a miracle in this girl's life. Not only can she run, she participated in a 5K race with her friends from school. Not only can she dance, she is part of the CLC Network Inclusive Dance Team. The same God who created majestic mountains tenderly caressed this child's brain so that we can see His work in her life. What an awesome God we serve!

Activity: Do you know of any person who has taught you that God works in our world? Retell that story and praise God for His might.

Prayer: Praise God for working in our world, and pray specifically for Him to work through the life of someone you know who has a disability.

Body Building

Day 3
Bringing Friends to Jesus

Bible Reading: Mark 2:1-12

Key Verse: "When Jesus saw their faith, He said to the paralytic, 'Son, your sins are forgiven.'" Mark 2:5

Devotional: Would you like to have been in that house when Jesus healed the man who could not walk? What an amazing thing it must have been to see him have his sins forgiven and then stand up and walk!

But what about the man's friends? I would like to have heard them talk. The Bible doesn't tell us about their conversation, but it could have gone something like this:

"Jesus is in there."

"Oh, if we could only get our friend to Jesus, I'm sure He would heal him."

"But it's so crowded."

"Hey, I have an idea. Let's take him up those stairs to the roof, make a hole in it, and lower him down right in front of Jesus."

"That's a great idea. Let's go."

When Jesus saw the faith of the paralyzed man and his friends, He healed him.

God wants our faith in Him to be strong, too. He has so many wonderful blessings for us, but it's our job to believe that God wants to work in our lives and the lives of those around us. This is another important gift that people with disabilities can give us – the building of a strong faith.

One of my students had many seizures. Her doctors had a hard time stopping them. Although they tried many different medicines, none of them was effective. When I talked to the mother of this young girl, she told me that throughout a very hard year the one thing they did not doubt was that God was with them guiding their lives. She said her faith was made much stronger because of her daughter's disability. What a wonderful gift this child gave to her whole family!

Many of you are friends with a person who has a disability. Does this person's life help you trust God more? Our faith must be like that of the paralyzed man's friends. Jesus also has the power to heal our friends, and we, too, can set them in front of Jesus. We can do that every day in our prayers.

Activity: There is another story in the Bible that talks about the faith of a friend as the reason for healing. Read Matthew 8:5-13.

Prayer: Put one of your friends in front of Jesus. You don't even need to make a hole in the roof to do so!

WEEK THREE

Day 4
Heart of Compassion

Bible Reading: Matthew 20:29-34

Key Verse: "Jesus had compassion on them and touched their eyes. Immediately they received their sight and followed Him." Matthew 20:34

Devotional: In our school, each child with a disability is in a general education classroom. The most exciting thing to watch in this inclusive education program is how a circle of friends develops around each person. The children learn to know one another and then take turns playing and working together.

One student at our school is a younger child who really enjoys playing ball and having fun with his friends. He also happens to be in a wheelchair. While he is getting stronger and learning to walk with a walker, he often goes outside to play in his wheelchair. He likes to play catch outside with his friends. One day, he tipped over in his wheelchair on the playground and got hurt. His friends were very concerned about him. While the ambulance came to school to make sure he was OK, the whole school seemed to jump into action. His friends started to pray. They made him cards to encourage him. Parents of his school friends made phone calls to find out how he was doing and if recovery was going well. The staff supported the family in a variety of ways. Each person saw the situation and God placed a heart of compassion in each one.

The opportunity to show compassion is another gift that people with disabilities can bring to a community. God instructs us to live a life of service, one that follows the patterns Jesus showed us. When He saw the two blind men, Jesus had compassion on them. In the same way, Jesus wants us to show compassion to the people in our lives. This certainly does not mean that we smother people who have a disability, doting on them and talking to them like children. It also does not mean that we are the only ones who can show compassion to others. Sometimes a person with a disability is the one who shows compassion to me. It does mean, however, that our hearts must feel compassion, and that where we can, we should support one another and help each person grow into the individual God intends him or her to be.

Compassion also means that we must not ridicule people with a disability. We must find ways to build each other up and not cut people down. It is our privilege to serve each person just as Jesus did. This is another wonderful gift we can develop as we support one another in the body of Christ.

Activity: Make a list of ways in which you could show compassion as a friend (not a smothering mother) to someone with a disability.

Prayer: Pray for a heart of compassion.

Body Building

Day 5
Praise God!

Bible Reading: Matthew 15:29-38

Key Verse: "The people were amazed when they saw the mute speaking, the crippled made well, the lame walking and the blind seeing. And they praised the God of Israel." Matthew 15:31

Devotional: I have a student who had a very bad accident a few years ago. He almost died. Thankfully, God saved his life. He was, however, very sick. He couldn't even walk or talk, and his doctors expected him to be in a wheelchair for the rest of his life. Well, the doctors were wrong. This child can now run on the playground and play with his friends. He can use a computer to talk for him, and is doing very well. Praise God, who can heal our bodies!

I remember a student who was in my very first class. He struggled for many years to do such things as match colors, say hello to me, and put on his boots. When we brought him in for tests, we were told that he had a severe cognitive impairment, that he would never read or write, and that he would need a lot of help. This student is now a teenager. His current teacher, led by God, began using a small keyboard with him. To my amazement, he spelled out "I am not an idiot." He now types about current events, math, and reading. Praise God, who can heal our minds!

Another student was born with cerebral palsy. She walks with a walker, and learning continues to be a struggle for her. A few years ago she told me that she had made profession of faith. She said that Jesus lives in her heart and that she is going to go to heaven. Praise God, who can heal our souls!

When you hear about God's work in the lives of these students, are you amazed? These, too, are miracles being done today. Do they make you want to praise God? When the people in the Bible saw Jesus perform miracles, they were amazed and praised God. I believe this is a gift that people with disabilities can give us. Their lives can point us to God, so that we can praise Him.

Activity: Rewrite the key verse for today so that it reflects the miracles you have seen in the lives of people with disabilities around you.

Prayer: Offer a prayer of praise in a sentence prayer. For what do you praise God today?

WEEK THREE

Day 6
We Are the Body of Christ

Bible Reading: 1 Corinthians 12:12-27
Key Verse: "Now you are the body of Christ, and each one of you is a part of it."
I Corinthians 12:27

Devotional: Years ago, most people born with a significant disability had to live in institutions. An institution is like a big hospital. Some of these institutions were very bad places, and the people who lived there were treated more like animals than like people. Other institutions were nicer, but even so, living away from home was very difficult for children. They couldn't stay with their own families or have their own bedrooms. The only people they lived with were other people with disabilities and the nurses who took care of them. Would you like to live that way?

How silly it would be, for example, if we decided that every person with glasses or contact lenses had to move into a big building together. They would have to sleep in large rooms with many beds. They would have to eat at long tables, and could not choose what they would eat. They could leave only for weekends, and only if a relative would come to take them out. You people who are wearing contacts and glasses would be very upset, I'm sure, especially if you were forced to go. That must be how people with disabilities felt when they were put in institutions.

Thankfully, there are not many of these institutions left. God intends for us to live together in our families and communities, without separating anyone who is different. God has led us to understand that we all need each other. People with disabilities help us to see God's work, to increase our faith, to have hearts of compassion, and to praise God. Why would we want to separate anyone who brings such gifts?

The Bible tells us that people with disabilities have been given a special place of honor in God's family. As Paul says in our passage for today (verses 24b-25), "But God has combined the members of the body and has given greater honor to the parts that lacked it, so that there should be no division in the body, but that its parts should have equal concern for each other." We must include each person in our Christian communities. Without such people in our schools, churches, and neighborhoods, we would be cheating ourselves out of an important part of God's gifts to us. I'm so thankful that I belong to a whole community, one which includes people with disabilities. They have taught me so much.

Activity: Talk about your church and school. Do they embrace differences, or do they want only certain people to be included? Would Jesus be happy with them?

Prayer: Pray for love in our communities so that all people can be accepted and celebrated as special gifts from God.

Body Building

Day 7
A Dream Come True

Bible Reading: Revelation 21:1-5

Key Verse: "He will wipe every tear from their eyes. There will be no more death or mourning or crying or pain, for the old order of things has passed away." Revelation 21:4

Devotional: What comes to mind when you think about heaven? Do you see angels, streets of gold, or choirs singing? Although each of us probably has a different idea of what heaven will be like, I would like to describe for you what some of my students are thinking about heaven.

I had three students around the table in my room. We were having a lesson about God's love for each of us. One of them, who has a vision impairment, looked up with great excitement and announced that she loves Jesus and is going to live with Him forever in heaven. I asked her what heaven would be like, and she said, "You know, Mrs. B., in heaven I will be able to see everything, and it will be beautiful. I am so excited."

The student sitting next to her can't speak, but he looked up at me, pointed to his mouth, made a grunt of excitement, and smiled. I said, "That's right. In heaven you're going to find me and tell me lots of stories." He nodded emphatically. I asked the student sitting next to him if he was going to heaven. He said, "No, I'm going home." When I assured him that his mom and dad would be in heaven too, he decided that he would go as well.

When we finished talking, we sang the song "Soon and Very Soon." We made up new verses like "We'll be talking there, we are going to see the King," and "We'll be seeing there, we are going to see the King."

Many of us look at ourselves and think we are pretty good people; we don't see too many problems. But God has healing to do in each of us. Whether that healing will be on the inside or the outside, God has exciting things in store for us as He makes us into a new creation.

Some of that healing God does right now on earth, and some of that healing will wait until we see Him in heaven. Whatever God's time may be for that healing in our lives, He promises to make a place where there will be no more sadness or sickness or dying or pain. Can you imagine that? What a beautiful promise God gives to us. Sign me up, I'm ready to go!

Activity: Make a big picture of heaven. Each person should draw a part that shows what he or she believes heaven will be like. Draw yourself in heaven, too. What will you look like?

Prayer: Praise God for heaven. Tell God again that you want Him to forgive your sins, and that you give Him your whole life just as He gave His life for you.

WEEK THREE

A Story of Your Own

Use this page to tell a story of your own. Is there a person in your life with a disability who has helped you see something in a new way? Tell that story here. Remember, if you would like to do so, follow the instructions in the back of this book and send it to us. We want to learn from your stories, too.

Bible Reading:

Key Verse:

Devotional:

Activity:

Prayer:

Body Building Workout: Week Four

Learning from the CLC Network Circle of Friends Drama Team

I want to introduce you to the CLC Network Circle of Friends Drama Team. Members of our current team include:

- Matthew and Jacob
- Rachel and Jaden
- Jonathan, Amber, and Kelsey
- John and Ryan
- Rosalyn and David

CLC Network is a partner organization that links arms with churches and schools as they build and promote inclusive and interdependent community. All of the children and young adults in the drama are or were part of one of our network Christian schools.

Circle of Friends is a term we use in schools to highlight and nurture the friendships between children with disabilities and their friends. Each person in the drama who has some sort of disability also has a friend in the cast. These friend pairs show how we work together to serve God.

Drama Team tells you what you will see. We perform a wordless drama because some of the members would really struggle to tell you about their love for Jesus given limited language abilities. They can, however, show you their commitment.

Over the past 10 years, I have had the opportunity to introduce this amazing group to worshipers gathered for churches, chapels and conferences in West Michigan and Iowa. While I am listed as the director of this team, they have taught me so very much. In fact, I often learn from those watching as well. While there is no written substitute for experiencing this drama in person, I do believe the group can teach us some important truths.

Barbara J. Newman

Copyright CLC Network 2009.

Day 1
The Drama: The Experience of Being Ministered To

Bible Reading: I Peter 4:7-11

Key Verse: "Each one should use whatever gift he has received to serve others, faithfully administering God's grace in its various forms." I Peter 4:10

Devotional: As the Christmas presents pile up under the tree, it's fun to take a peek at the tags. "To John, From Dad." "To Dad, From Jim." From reading those short phrases, it's clear to tell who is receiving the gift and who is giving the gift.

Sometimes at Christmas, our family chooses to purchase gifts for a person who doesn't have much money. We shop together and put all the wrapped items in a box for that person to receive. We do not expect this person to give any gifts to us in return, because that person doesn't have the money to buy presents.

I have seen people treat a person with a disability similar to the way we give gifts at Christmas to a person with very little money. They figure that a person with a disability should only receive gifts because that person doesn't have any gifts to give to someone else. Our Bible verses today, as well as the drama team members themselves, remind us that this is not true! God has given each one of His children a gift to share with other people. Not only can we give God's gifts to a person with a disability, but we can expect that person to give a gift back to us.

One of my favorite parts of the drama team performance is watching how people react. As God speaks through this group and touches the hearts and minds of people watching, it is clear that many have never had the experience of receiving a gift that God wants to give through a person with a disability. Each drama team member is using the gifts God has given to him or her to serve the worshipping community. Not only does this wordless drama tell the story of salvation and the sacrifice of the physical body of Christ, the team also works together to tell the story of the body of Christ – His church. The drama team is the "minister," bringing the message God wants to deliver to His children.

Activity: Think of a time when you have given a gift (ministered to) a person with a disability. Also think of a time when you have received a gift from a person with a disability.

Prayer: Thank you, Lord, for the gift of salvation that opens the doors for each one of us to enter into your family. We praise you for the body of Christ and the way we can minister to each other through the gifts you have given us to share. In Jesus' name, amen.

Body Building

Day 2
Friend Pairs

Bible Reading: Exodus 4:1-17

Key Verses: "You shall speak to him and put words in his mouth; I will help both of you speak and will teach you what to do. He will speak to the people for you, and it will be as if he were your mouth and as if you were God to him." Exodus 4:15-16

Devotional: We had the joy of traveling with our drama team on a tour to Iowa. Not only was it a great way to share the message of this drama with people in another state, we had the chance to have some great fun together. Each member of the drama team with a disability is paired up with at least one friend, and I got to watch these pairs in action for a whole week.

When one person with Down Syndrome needed ear plugs for the hotel pool in Illinois, the friend was right there to make sure it happened. When another person was hesitant to go in to the whirlpool, a friend with Autism was right there to encourage bravery. While one person was a bit shy around strangers, a friend with a Cognitive Impairment came alongside and shared the good news of Jesus with another swimmer at the hotel. The luggage all ended up in the right places, the props were carefully set up, and the drama team used the gifts and supported the needs of each person there. They served one another as they carried the good news of Jesus Christ around the state of Iowa.

These friend pairs remind me of a story in the Bible. God had given Moses a huge assignment. God would equip him to take on Pharaoh and lead God's children out of Egypt. Moses was less than confident about this idea. One concern Moses had was in his ability to speak to other people. He tells God in verse 10, "O Lord, I have never been eloquent, neither in the past nor since you have spoken to your servant. I am slow of speech and tongue." God chose to assign Moses a partner. Moses would receive the words and instructions from God, pass them on to his brother Aaron, and Aaron would do the talking. It was a God-designed partnership.

For whatever reason, when God was designing each one of us, He made us with areas that are easy for us. These are our strengths. Every person also has areas that are difficult. These are our weaknesses. It seems that God wants us to partner up – He made us so that we can use our strengths to help someone else and then receive help from someone for our areas of weakness. We are made to fit together.

Activity: Get a piece of paper and cut it in half, making the cut mark look like the end of a puzzle piece. Draw yourself on one half of that paper and draw a friend you help and who helps you back on the other half of the paper. You fit together like a puzzle!

Prayer: Thank God for the gifts He gives you to share with others, as well as the friends He gives you to help in the areas that are more difficult for you.

WEEK FOUR

Day 3
Introducing: Jonathan

Bible Reading: Ephesians 2:1-10
Key Verse: "For we are God's workmanship, created in Christ Jesus to do good works, which God prepared in advance for us to do." Ephesians 2:10

Devotional: If you are ever having a rough day – a day where you are thinking that there is nothing very special about you, remember this verse. The Bible says that you are "God's workmanship." God made you; He handcrafted you and has important jobs for you to do in His Kingdom. Just like an artist autographs her work, God is the artist who made you. Imagine that somewhere on your body is a tattoo that says, "Handmade by God." That makes you a very special and amazing person.

While I could tell you about any one of our drama team members, I want to introduce you to Jonathan. He was born long enough ago that when the doctor saw that Jonathan had Down Syndrome, he told Jonathan's parents to expect him to live away from his family – in an institution. Jonathan's parents, however, saw God's "tattoo" on his body and knew that God would use Jonathan in important ways in His kingdom. They took him home.

I met Jonathan in school when he was very young. He was a student in my first class. I didn't know God's exact plan for his life, but I trusted that Jonathan was handmade by God and that He had important work for him to do.

Jonathan grew into an amazing young man who is passionate about God and serving Him. He is sensitive to the needs of others, often offering to pray with a person who might be having a tough day. He cries over the hurts of others and laughs at joyful times. Jonathan is a loyal and faithful friend, and relationships with God and others are at the top of his list.

When we started doing this drama, it was clear that God had groomed Jonathan to play the role of Jesus. He feels the distress of those trapped in sin as he prays over them. He struggles through the pain and agony that Jesus must have felt in His death. He takes great joy in welcoming each person into the waiting arms of Jesus, who clothes them with new life.

I am so thankful that Jonathan's parents recognized God's "tattoo" the day he was born. Jonathan, along with each one of you, is God's work of art, and He has an important plan for your life.

Activity: Write out the key verse for today on a note card. Stick it on your bathroom mirror. Put your face above it and remember every day who you are!

Prayer: Thank you, Lord, for the way you designed each one of us. Show us those jobs you have for us to do. We want to serve you. In Jesus' name, amen.

Body Building

Day 4
The Curbside Show

Bible Reading: Romans 8:28-39
Key Verse: "And we know that in all things God works for the good of those who love Him, who have been called according to His purpose." Romans 8:28

Devotional: No trip would be complete without an adventure story. When our drama team went to Iowa, we certainly returned with a tale to tell. We were almost to our final destination at Dordt College. We pulled the bus into a Burger King parking lot about an hour away so that we could arrive with full stomachs. After we enjoyed our burgers and fries, the whole group hopped on the bus, waiting to finish the journey. As the bus driver tried to get the vehicle to start, a giant puff of black smoke came from the tail pipe. That bus was not moving! We were stuck.

Our verse for today tells us that "God works for the good of those who love Him," and this night was no exception. As the drama team went back inside Burger King to pray, the bus driver noticed a small crowd on the other side of the road. Knowing the bus was out of commission, he ventured over only to find out that they were having a prayer vigil outside the building. They were praying because this building was a place where many people went when thinking about having an abortion. The bus driver quickly gathered up the drama team and offered to add to the prayer vigil by performing this drama on the curb of Burger King, directly across from this building.

We popped our CD into a car stereo, pulled the props and costumes off the ailing bus, and went to perform our drama for those who were praying, as well as those who were considering an abortion. The team communicated clearly the love of Jesus and the way to freedom from sin. As we were finishing up the drama, it was clear that God wanted to use the broken-down bus adventure to minister to the people in this town. He picked us to tell the salvation story. He picked us to give a clear message about the value of each person and how each one is a treasure to God. May that message be forever etched on that curbside in Iowa.

Activity: Can you think of a time when something unexpected or bad happened, but God turned it into something really good? Tell that story.

Prayer: Pray Romans 8:38-39 out loud for a prayer today. We praise you and thank you, God. "For I am convinced that neither death nor life, neither angels nor demons, neither the present nor the future, nor any powers, neither height nor depth, nor anything else in all creation, will be able to separate us from the love of God that is in Christ Jesus our Lord." Amen!

WEEK FOUR

Day 5
But It Looks So Pretty!

Bible Reading: James 1:2-18
Key Verses: "But each one is tempted when, by his own evil desire, he is dragged away and enticed. Then, after desire has conceived, it gives birth to sin; and sin, when it is full-grown, gives birth to death." James 1:14-15

Devotional: The evil dessert tray. In many restaurants you have a chance to eat a wonderful meal, and then the server says, "Would you care for some dessert?" While it's relatively easy to say "no" at this point in the conversation, the restaurant is ready and willing to add those last calories to your bill. The server, not taking "no" for an answer, wanders over with a dessert tray or cart. These magnificent sweet creations stare you in the face, almost asking you to pick one to eat. Once you see and smell those wonderful desserts, it's much more difficult to say "no." Hmm…maybe you could split one with a friend.

Part of the drama is a reminder that sin can come packaged up with very pretty ribbon. It's like that tempting dessert tray that looks so wonderful, but often it is a bad choice. The drama members have a chance to choose between two boxes, one quite plain and the other wrapped up like a big, beautiful birthday present. Inside that box, however, is the pull into sin. Satan uses money, fame, jewels, music, and more to pull us in to a place where we soon get caught by sin. Once we are caught, there is nothing we can do to escape on our own. It's at that point in the drama when Jesus enters in to that place of darkness to bring God's plan of salvation.

I was attending a conference. The speaker was a woman with Autism, and it was time for questions. One mom raised her hand and said, "I have a daughter with Autism, and I want to know the best way to help her understand about Jesus." The speaker, who is not a Christian, answered the only way she knew how. She quickly said, "God is too hard for people with Autism to understand. Next question." That mom was devastated. She started to cry. Could it be true that her daughter might not have a chance to know Jesus? As I was trying to get close enough to that mom to give her a different answer, a picture of the drama came in to my mind. As the people are trapped in sin, God sends His son Jesus into the picture to place His hand on each person and feels that person's pain and darkness. I wanted to tell this mom, "It's not about what your daughter knows. It's that God knows your daughter and loves her very much. He designed her, and wants her as His child. She can choose to respond to that gift." As my friend with Autism noted, "My body might have Autism, but my soul does not." This is her way of saying that there is no disability in the way she knows and loves Jesus.

Praise God for sending His Son into our world and each one of our lives.

Activity: Our Bible verse says that there are things that entice us and drag us away from God. Have you ever felt that?

Prayer: Ask God to forgive you and protect you from sin and those things that drag you away from God.

Body Building

Day 6
Coming Under the Cloth

Bible Reading: Philippians 2:1-11

Key Verses: "…that at the name of Jesus every knee should bow, in heaven and on earth and under the earth, and every tongue confess that Jesus Christ is Lord, to the glory of God the Father." Philippians 2:10-11

Devotional: One of the drama props we use is a large red cloth. It's used in many different ways. As the drama team member portraying Jesus is dying on the cross, we drape that cloth around his neck to remember that Jesus bled and died for us. When we lay Jesus in the grave, the red cloth covers him up. When we see Jesus rise, that red cloth is lifted off of him and then becomes a gate. As the drama participants each give his or her life to Jesus, they bow before him and then each one walks under that red cloth – a symbol of the blood of Jesus – and into the loving arms of the Savior.

At the end of the drama, we sometimes have the congregation sing a song while we invite anyone watching to come under that red cloth and receive a hug from the actor who plays the role of Jesus. It is a reminder that Jesus has washed away the sins of that person as well as a way to remember that each one who believes in Jesus and receives salvation is a member of the body of Christ.

One of the joys as the director of the drama is to watch the line of people coming under that cloth. Some people have accepted Christ as Savior for the very first time after seeing the drama. Others are remembering that Jesus died for his or her sins. The line of people walking under that red cloth has included seminary professors, young children, people in wheelchairs, people representing many cultures and races, English speakers, and non-English speakers. At one chapel service, an elderly man held the hand of a young child with Autism as they walked together under the cloth and into the arms of Jesus.

Jesus has a very large family with so many different kinds of people. Even though we are all very different, we all agree on one very important thing. We agree that "every knee should bow… and every tongue confess that Jesus Christ is Lord!"

Activity: Do you have a red towel or cloth? Give everyone in your group a chance to hold it or walk under it. Remember that Jesus died for you and that He loves you.

Prayer: Tell Jesus about your love for Him. Thank God for the other members of His giant family.

WEEK FOUR

Day 7
Van Andel Arena and Curbside Shows

Bible Reading: Colossians 3:18-25

Key Verses: "Whatever you do, work at it with all your heart, as working for the Lord, not for men, since you know that you will receive an inheritance from the Lord as a reward. It is the Lord Christ you are serving." Colossians 3:23-24

Devotional: One highlight for our drama team was to participate in a large celebration that took place at the Van Andel Arena, a very large facility. The seats were sold out as this team took the stage. There was a camera person bobbing up and down in front of the group so the images could also be put up on the arena screens. Thousands of people and bobbing cameras might tend to make someone a bit nervous. I know several of my fingernails got shorter the night before the performance, but the drama team had their nerves firmly under control.

As the director, I take the requests for scheduling the drama team. I know a lot about who will be in attendance. We have had the honor of presenting the drama to many different groups, and the most recent performance had me a bit nervous. The group consisted of worship leaders, many whose names you might recognize. One member of the audience was very well-known for his skill in playing the piano. The seating arrangement placed one of our drama members immediately next to the piano. As the accomplished musician began to play, the song built in intensity and beauty. The drama member, who happens to have Down Syndrome, leaned far back in his seat to catch a glimpse of these skilled fingers quickly moving up and down the keyboard. The young man leaned over to me, shrugged, and said, "He's pretty good, don't ya think?"

That statement, in addition to making me smile, was another reminder to focus my attention on the most important audience. While I can be tempted to think too much about the people present and the positions they may hold, the drama team seems to be quite oblivious to the number of people in the audience, bobbing cameras, and academic titles. In fact, the drama performance would be the same whether given at the Van Andel Arena or on the curbside at Burger King. How I treasure this focus on God as our audience. It allows the group members to be available for what God might want to do with those in attendance.

When we were done with the drama that night at the worship conference, a particularly beautiful picture entered my mind. I couldn't help but think about Jesus leaning over and saying about both the gifted pianist and the gifted Christian drama group, "They're pretty good, don't ya think?" It is always our hope and prayer that God is honored because of the drama and the precious members who make up the team.

Activity: What gifts has God given you? Do you play the piano? Read well? Show people care when they are hurting? Imagine those things and then think about those areas as a gift to God. Consider drawing a picture or writing about those things and wrapping them in a pretty package as a reminder that it belongs to God.

Prayer: "Lord, thank you for making me good at _____. I want to do that just for you.

Body Building

A Story of Your Own

Use this page to tell a story of your own. Is there a person in your life with a disability who has helped you see a Bible verse or story in a new way? Tell that story here. Remember, if you would like to do so, follow the instructions in the back of this book and send it to us. We want to learn from your stories, too.

Bible Reading:

Key Verse:

Devotional:

Activity:

Prayer:

Body Building Workout: Week Five

Learning from Marie

I invite you to meet my friend Marie.

Marie's Areas of Strength: Marie is a woman with amazing joy. It radiates from her smile and eyes when she interacts with people. She is good at reading and scanning words quickly. She also enjoys a good laugh and is passionate about serving Jesus. She is committed to praying for others and keeps all prayer requests completely confidential.

Marie's Areas of Need: Marie is unable to voluntarily move any of her body parts except for her eyes and some additional facial muscles. She cannot use spoken words to communicate and depends on caregivers for meeting her basic needs each day.

Marie's Story: Marie lives in a group home across the street from my church. She is in her 40s and really enjoys being part of the church community. Caregivers wheel her over in her chair on Sundays, as well as other times during the week. There are people in our church who know how to help Marie should the need arise, but these same people know how to tap into Marie's gifts so she can use them as part of our gathering each week. She has a G.L.U.E. team (a trained group of individuals who come around Marie as friends), and she teaches me something new every time I am around her. I understand God differently because of my friendship with Marie.

Marie's Hope and Barb's Hope for the Church: Just as we have become friends in Christ, it is our hope that other church communities will experience the gifts and support the needs of others with disabilities so that the body of Christ may be more complete.

Barbara J. Newman

Copyright CLC Network 2009.

Body Building

Day 1
Surprising Marie

Bible Reading: I Samuel 16:1-13

Key Verse: "But the Lord said to Samuel, 'Do not consider his appearance or his height, for I have rejected him. The Lord does not look at the things man looks at. Man looks at the outward appearance, but the Lord looks at the heart.'" I Samuel 16:7

Devotional: I understand how Samuel made his mistake. He went to Jesse's house looking for a king. In his mind, a king had certain features. Samuel was probably thinking about tall and handsome Saul, looking for those same characteristics in one of Jesse's sons. As the sons paraded past, Samuel was only looking through his own eyes. Sometimes I forget that there is a different pair of "eyeglasses" from God that I can use. Those are the "glasses" God wanted Samuel to use.

I made the same mistake as Samuel the first time I met Marie. She came to my church one day and I saw a woman in a wheelchair. I could tell from the way she was positioned that it was very hard for this person to move at all. Not only that, I tried to speak to her, but she just looked at me and smiled. I quickly moved away, not sure what else to say or do. When I left church that day, all I knew about Marie was her "outward appearance." I didn't remember to use God's "eyeglasses" to really see this person. What I saw was a disability.

Now that Marie and I have been friends for several years, I don't really even see her wheelchair anymore. It's there, and sometimes she asks me to move it around, but when I see Marie at church, I am thinking about a woman with a great sense of humor who has a passionate love for Jesus. When I see Marie, I see a gifted intercessor who brings life and warmth almost immediately into any setting. Over time, God has given me His "eyeglasses" to see Marie. While many people still get stuck looking only at Marie's outward appearance, I have had the joy of being able to see her heart. I praise God for that view.

Maybe you can remember a time when you met a person with a disability. It might have been a person who looked or acted a bit differently. Don't make the same mistake I made with Marie! Remember to put on God's "eyeglasses" and see a person who is made in the image of God – someone He loves very much. Remember to see a person who was handmade by God before that person was even born. That person has strengths as well as areas of need – just like you. God's "glasses" will help you see that.

Activity: Practice using God's "eyeglasses." Look at someone in the room right now and see how very much God loves that person. Look at that individual's gifts, personality, and interests. Look beyond the person's clothes or hair color and see that person's heart.

Prayer: Lord, we want to have your eyes when we look at other people. Help us to see what you see. In Jesus' name, amen.

WEEK FIVE

Day 2
The Power of Information

Bible Reading: John 8:1-11

Key Verse: "When they kept on questioning Him, He straightened up and said to them, 'If any one of you is without sin, let him be the first to throw a stone at her.'" John 8:7

Devotional: This is one of my favorite stories about God's "eyeglasses." The people who were about to stone this woman saw only one thing – adultery. She had done something that deserved punishment, and they were about to kill her for this crime. Their focus was only on her sin, and they had rules for how to handle this. Jesus, however, had a different view. In one sentence, he challenged people to see the situation a completely different way. "If any one of you is without sin, let him be the first to throw a stone at her." He handed out a new pair of "eyeglasses" to each person holding a stone. Instead of looking at her, they saw the sinfulness in their own lives. The Bible says that starting with the older men, they all dropped their stones and left. Jesus then had a chance to speak to this woman, expressing His acceptance of her as well as reminding her to make better choices.

Many times, I see that passing out God's "eyeglasses" to people can be very helpful. In fact, this is a great way in schools, churches, and homes to better understand a person with a disability. When someone gives me new information, I can see that person in a different way. One of the most helpful things for me was visiting with people who knew Marie. I wanted to see more than a wheelchair, and they helped me understand how to communicate with Marie. They told me her story and they taught me how to use her communication board. I found out that Marie could use her eyes to scan a page of words. As my finger traced over columns and rows, Marie would look at me to stop my finger from moving. We used this system to build phrases and sentences. I found out that Marie is very smart. Even though she can't move her body much, she can think very well. I can also ask Marie yes and no questions. She uses her eyes to tell me the answers. Once I found out this information about Marie, it helped me use God's "eyeglasses."

Our church decided that many people should know about Marie. We asked her caregivers to train us. We used printed information and brief training sessions to let people know how Marie communicates and tell about her story. Of course, first we asked for Marie's permission. When she looked at us and smiled, we knew her answer was "yes."

Activity: Can you think of a person in your church, school, or home that you don't understand very well? Think of a way you can better understand this person's story. Perhaps you could call a family member or invite that person out for dinner or coffee. Before you meet, ask God to give you His "eyeglasses" to better see this person.

Prayer: Thinking of that same person, pray for him or her. Then pray that God would also give you His "eyeglasses" for this person.

Body Building

Day 3
Hilarious Giving

Bible Reading: Matthew 5:13-16

Key Verse: "In the same way, let your light shine before men, that they may see your good deeds and praise your Father in heaven." Matthew 5:16

Devotional: I thought they liked us. After all, we are a church. Marie's group home is located right across the street from our church, and I thought most people liked churches. What I didn't know is that when Marie first started coming to our church, her caregivers didn't like us at all.

While our church had not been unkind to them, they had heard many stories about churches and people with disabilities. In fact, lots of people know these stories. They know about people who have been hurt because a church asked that person with Autism to leave and try a different church. The caregivers had heard stories from another person in a wheelchair who wanted to go to church, but the only place a wheelchair could fit was in the church basement. The people at the church didn't seem to care about that. There are so many other stories about people with disabilities being sent away, asked to leave, ignored, and ridiculed. Of all the places where people should be received with honor and respect, some churches don't seem to be able to use God's eyes.

We wanted Marie's group home to have a new story to tell about churches and people with disabilities. We needed a way to tell them that our church would welcome, respect, and honor Marie as a dearly loved child of God. We had a visiting pastor talk to us about money. He suggested we participate in something termed "hilarious giving." This was a chance for people to enjoy giving an offering to God that came straight from the heart. Well, our church was hilarious alright. That offering brought in thousands of dollars. We prayed about how to use that offering, and one of the decisions we made was to bless Marie's home. While they tried hard to make ends meet with the money they received from the State, it was hard. Marie needed an updated wheelchair, the doors to the kitchen needed to be wider, and the home desperately needed air conditioning. There were inside and outside repairs that our deacons could do, and we were able to spend many hours updating and renovating Marie's home. Our children's ministry decided to bless the residents of the home with Christmas presents that year. When we were done, the staff at that home – not typically churchgoers – would not only drop Marie off for worship on Sundays, they started to attend church as well. We became good neighbors. As we began to shine the light of Jesus into that home, they could tell we had a different story to tell them.

Activity: Do you have a group home in your neighborhood? Do you know of a family that might not be able to get out much because of a family member with a disability? Let your church, school, or family communicate a new story about Christians. Show your respect, care, and love by letting the light of Jesus shine through you.

Prayer: Add that home to your prayer list. If possible, find out specific ways you can pray for people. Sometimes rules of confidentiality might get in the way, but remember that God knows the needs, and you can still pray over that home.

WEEK FIVE

Day 4
Gifted Marie

Bible Reading: Romans 12:1-8

Key Verses: "…so in Christ we who are many form one body, and each member belongs to all the others. We have different gifts, according to the grace given us." Romans 12:5-6a

Devotional: Imagine that you have stickers on your arms. For every area that is easy for you (strengths), you have a green sticker. For the areas that are hard for you (weaknesses), you have a pink sticker. If you are a fast runner and a good reader, you would have a green sticker for each of those areas. If doing math and remembering phone numbers are hard for you, you would have a pink sticker for each of those areas. When God designed us, He seemed to make us with both green and pink areas. We all have things that are easy for us and things that are more difficult.

Sometimes, when people look at an individual with a disability, they might only see pink stickers. They might think about the areas that are hard for that person and figure that person must be all pink. Sometimes people do that with my friend, Marie. They see a person who can't use her legs or arms, a person who can't talk, and a person who needs help doing practically everything. Pink Marie, they see. I am here to tell you, however, that the Bible disagrees. God does not make "all pink" people.

Romans 12 tells us that we all have different gifts, and we belong to one another. Places where I am strong, I can help you. Places where you are strong, you can help me. I know that God designed Marie with green and pink areas; the same is true for any one of us. Marie communicates concern and care for others through her expressive eyes and face. Her joy is contagious. She is also faithful in praying for others. Many will mention prayer requests to Marie who will then pray for these situations during the week. The church sends an e-mail to a staff person at her home with weekly prayer requests from members of the church so that Marie can pray. Marie and all the others at my church belong to one another and we share the gifts that God has put inside each person, including green and pink Marie.

Activity: Think about a person you know who has a disability. Instead of thinking about the areas that are hard for that person, make a list of the gifts and strengths that person has to offer others.

Prayer: Dear Lord, thank you for your design in each one of us. Thank you for making us fit together so that we all belong to one another. Help us to use our gifts to serve others, and help us to receive the gifts that others bring. In Jesus' name, amen.

Body Building

Day 5
Heart Singing

Bible Reading: Ephesians 5:15-21

Key Verse: "Speak to one another with psalms, hymns and spiritual songs. Sing and make music in your heart to the Lord." Ephesians 5:19

Devotional: One of my favorite times in church is group singing. I love to join with many other voices to praise God. Melody, harmony, with instruments or voices only, I enjoy singing about my love for God. Sometimes, however, I find myself thinking about the voice of the person behind me or what I had for breakfast or what movie I might watch in the afternoon. I am distracted by my thoughts or how a worship leader might be moving or singing. Thinking about my own life or the way my neighbor sounds, I've soon lost the point of worship. What started as singing to praise God turned into a rambling package of thoughts and ideas.

Marie, however, taught me to think about singing time very differently. She is a "joyful noise" variety of singer. Every once in awhile she can open her mouth and a sound comes out during worship time, but mostly she participates in singing by making "music in your heart to the Lord." Marie's time of worship is spent forming her thoughts, ideas and love for God inside her heart. She has a primarily silent time of making music, and I know it must be a very beautiful song to God. While I'm sure Marie can get distracted by off-key singers, a squealing sound system, or a string that just popped off someone's guitar, I also know she understands very clearly the point of singing time. She tunes her heart instrument to make music for God, and voice or no voice, she communicates her love and praise to God. When I find myself getting distracted and wandering away from God, I remember Marie and how important it is for me to begin my song to God in my heart and let everything else come out from that place.

I often wonder how Marie and I will communicate in heaven. Will she have a voice then? Will it be a high or low voice? Or will my voice be more like hers – where I can sing and make music in my heart to God? Whatever God has in store for us, I know that my sister in Christ and I will be able to blend our voices to praise Jesus.

Activity: Think of a song you like to sing to praise God. Before you begin, pretend that you are in Marie's body and get your heart song in tune before you start singing out loud. Focus on your love for God and having a conversation with Him first, and then sing from your heart.

Prayer: Use that praise song as your prayer time. Make it a beautiful song of praise to the God who made you, loves you, and sent Jesus so that you can be His child forever.

Day 6
Creative Communion

Bible Reading: I Corinthians 11:23-26
Key Verse: "For whenever you eat this bread and drink this cup, you proclaim the Lord's death until He comes." I Corinthians 11:26

Devotional: Remember this sequence of numbers and repeat it back without looking: 2-7-9-3 (repeat that set of numbers). Try repeating this: 5-3-9-0-1 (repeat that set of numbers). Now attempt to repeat this set of numbers: 4-6-8-1-4-2 (repeat that set of numbers). Finally, try to remember this sequence: 6-0-2-3-6-9-7-1-5-0 (repeat that set of numbers).

Sometimes, it's hard to remember a list of numbers or words, especially when it gets too long. When the list is long, some people write it down on a piece of paper. If, for example, you need to get seven items from the grocery store, it might help to make a written list. If you need to remember a longer set of numbers or words, you might want to make up a song for those items. Those memory tools can be very helpful.

God put a memory tool in the Bible for us. It's called Communion or the Lord's Supper. He wants us to remember Jesus, and so He tells us that "whenever you eat this bread and drink this cup, you proclaim the Lord's death until He comes." The bread and juice help us remember that Jesus loves us, died for us, and is coming back for us.

In our church, we take communion and remember Jesus by walking to the front of the worship center where someone gives us a piece of bread and holds out a cup of juice where we dip the bread. It's important to us that everyone who believes in Jesus has a chance to remember Him, so we want Marie to participate as well. Sometimes churches need to be creative, so we asked Marie's caregivers to help us figure it out. When Marie asks to take communion by telling us with her eyes, we push her wheelchair to the front of church. The server breaks off a small piece of bread and gets it very wet in the juice cup. The server tells her "The body of Christ broken for you" and "The blood of Christ poured out for you." Then Marie opens her mouth and sticks out her tongue. The soggy bread is placed far back on her tongue by the server and Marie takes communion, too. We all remember Jesus together.

Activity: If Marie went to your church, how could she take communion along with everyone else? What kind of creative plan would you have for her? If Marie wanted to greet other people during greeting time or passing of the peace, what creative plan would you use then?

Prayer: Remember Jesus in your prayer time today. Remember what He did for you and talk to Him about the gift of salvation.

Body Building

Day 7
Family of Believers

Bible Reading: Galatians 6:1-10

Key Verse: "Therefore, as we have opportunity, let us do good to all people, especially to those who belong to the family of believers." Galatians 6:10

Devotional: Marie has many friends at our church. Not only does she have friends while at church, but she enjoys friendships during the week. One family built a ramp into their home so Marie and one of her caregivers could come over for supper. This entire family really got close to her over the years. Marie started to call the father of this family her dad. In fact, they acted so much like a family together that Marie decided to make it official. She changed her last name so that she was a legal member of this family group.

When we become Christians, we have a name change too. God adopts us as His children. The Bible verse for today assumes that all Christians "belong to the family of believers." Just as Marie now calls Bill her father, Christians have a heavenly father. Marie has official brothers and sisters as part of Bill's family, and Christians have new brothers and sisters as well. In fact, if you are a Christian, you are related through Jesus to Marie and to me.

Marie is part of my church family in Michigan. God gave her as a gift to us, and we are so thankful to know her and grow together with her in Christ. I am guessing, however, that Marie might remind you of someone in your church or school home. While your friend's story might be a bit different, think about how you might best grow together as a family.

Can you get to know that person like we enjoy knowing Marie? How can you talk to that person? Can you find ways to be creative so that person can be more a part of your community? How can you help that person and how can that person help you? I know your church or school can tell a new story to your town about how you want to show honor and respect to people with disabilities. Be God's light in your town as you follow God's directions in our verse for today. "Therefore, as we have opportunity, let us do good to all people, especially to those who belong to the family of believers."

Activity: Sometimes families take a family picture. Mom and Dad, brothers and sisters, children, grandchildren, and others might be included in the photograph. Imagine taking a family picture of God's family. Think about who would be included in that photo. Don't forget Marie! She's in the picture, too.

Prayer: Choose someone from God's family picture to pray for today.

A Story of Your Own

Marie is my special friend from church. Maybe you have a special friend from church or school. Introduce us to your friend. Remember, if you would like to do so, follow the instructions in the back of this book and send it to us. We want to learn from your stories. If it's OK with your friend, include a picture, too.

Introduction: Meet

's Areas of Strength:

's Areas of Need:

's Story:

's Hope for the Church:

Body Building Workout: Week Six

Learning from Friendships

From the beginning years of life to the ending years, friends are a gift from God that we cherish. Think about your week. How many times have you talked to or been with a friend? Did you play with someone at school or in your neighborhood? Did you talk to a friend on the phone or meet someone for coffee? Did you communicate with a friend on Facebook or through mail or email? God places individuals in our lives as friends to encourage us, help us, entertain us, and give life more meaning.

Biblical examples of friendships abound, making clear that this gift has been around for a long time. David and Jonathan, Paul and Silas, and Jesus and his disciples (Jesus says to them in John 15:15, "I no longer call you servants…instead, I have called you friends") are just a few examples of the way God highlights friendships and partnerships in Scripture.

Working in inclusive environments has taught me a lot about friendships with persons who have disabilities. Many individuals suffer from a lack of friends. One important goal of inclusive schools and churches is to build friendships through a Circle of Friends (schools) and G.L.U.E. teams (churches). As relationships develop, it's clear to see that the benefit of a friendship is never a one-way street. Each person in the friendship grows as they help one another and spend time together.

This set of devotions lists a few things I have learned from watching friendships between persons with disabilities and their peers from school and churches. These examples include both children and adults.

It is my prayer that your life may be enriched by friendships such as these.

Barbara J. Newman

Copyright CLC Network 2009.

Day 1
Puzzle Pieces

Bible Reading: I Corinthians 12:12-20
Key Verse: "But in fact God has arranged the parts in the body, every one of them, just as He wanted them to be." I Corinthians 12:18

Devotional: When we moved into our home, some friends gave us a housewarming party. We opened up several gifts. Every time we opened a new present, I started to picture where that item might go in the new home. Would I put that tea kettle on a display shelf in the kitchen, or would it go on the stove? Would that handmade quilt go over the arm of the couch in the living room, or would it go in one of the bedrooms? Not only was each item a gift, I also had the chance to arrange the gifts in our home.

We know from Scripture that God designs each person. He chooses what color hair and eyes that person will have. He knits together that person's physical appearance as well as a unique personality and gift mix. If that is not special enough, the Bible verse tells us that God then ARRANGES that person. In other words, just as I was able to choose the perfect spot for each item in my home, God gets to arrange His people. He arranges them into families and neighborhoods and churches. The people He has placed in your life are not there by accident or chance. God is the master creator and arranger.

Sometimes I like to think about people as puzzle pieces. On our puzzle piece you will find all the special things about us – things we are good at, things that are difficult for us. Sometimes I wonder why God didn't make us to be good at everything. That would seem to make life much easier. But I suspect God had an important plan even in that part of how we are made. If each one of us could do everything well, we really wouldn't need each other all that much. God designed our puzzle piece so that we would want and need to hook up with other puzzle pieces. I can help someone where they struggle, and that person can help me. If you put all of God's puzzle pieces together, we make up the body of Christ – God's giant puzzle.

When God sends a new person to a church or school, it's like He is giving you a gift. He knows you are missing a puzzle piece, and that person will make you more complete. As you use the gifts and support the needs of that individual, the body of Christ becomes stronger. As we look at friendships this week, consider the special ways these puzzle pieces are hooked together. Praise God for His arrangements.

Prayer: Think about the people that God has arranged in your life. These might be family members, friends, or neighbors. How many puzzle pieces do you have attached to your piece? Think of one person in your puzzle that is especially helpful and encouraging to you. Pray for that person today.

Body Building

Day 2
Summer SERVE

Bible Reading: Philippians 1:3-11

Key Verses: "In all my prayers for all of you, I always pray with joy because of your partnership in the gospel from the first day until now." Philippians 1:4-5

Devotional: Summer time is special for many reasons. You can enjoy the warm weather, swimming, vacation time, gardening, and fireworks. Maybe you spend part of your summer camping. Others of you might enjoy boat rides or amusement parks. One very special part of my summer is called Summer SERVE. I look forward to it every year.

God asks us to use our gifts to serve Him and others. Since we all have gifts, it makes sense that each one of us should find a way to serve. Every summer in Zeeland, Michigan, young adults with disabilities meet up with a friend for the week and participate in service projects all around this community. They have worked together in pairs to paint barns, babysit children, do lawn work, cook meals for those without homes to live in, and help out around the community any way they are needed. I have the joy of being the evening speaker for this week-long camp as we grow together while serving others.

Bekki is one of the people at Summer SERVE. She comes each year to help with the small groups. She also happens to be in a wheelchair. In order for Bekki to use her gifts of teaching about Jesus and praying for others, she needs a partner. That partner, Rachel, helps her get showered, dressed, and opens the containers at mealtimes for her so that she is able to use the gifts God has given her. In return, Rachel will be able to benefit from Bekki's small group leading. I always look at Bekki and her friend Rachel as an example of a "partnership in the gospel." Bekki needs Rachel and Rachel needs Bekki. They are partners because they know people need to hear about the good news of Jesus Christ.

Bekki and Rachel represent one partnership at Summer SERVE this year. There are 37 other pairs of people who have chosen to partner together. Look out, Zeeland Michigan! I can't wait to see what God will do through these friends.

Prayer: Lord God, you have asked each one of us to use our gifts to serve you and others. Show us how we might partner with others to bring the good news of Jesus Christ to our community. In Jesus' name, amen.

Day 3
Michelle and Melissa

Bible Reading: Romans 12:9-13
Key Verse: "Share with God's people who are in need. Practice hospitality." Romans 12:13

Devotional: Moving to a new state can be exciting and scary all at the same time. It might be exciting to get to meet new people, move to a new home, and start a new job or school. It also might be scary, especially if you don't know many people in the new town. That's what happened to my friend Michelle.

Michelle got a new job, so she and her family moved to Holland, Michigan. They didn't have any relatives or friends here, so they worked hard to meet neighbors as well as choose a new church home. Many times, churches are a great place to meet new friends. Unfortunately, that didn't happen right away for Michelle.

Her family visited a church for several weeks, and people were not very friendly to her. Most people, that is. There was one person who made a point to meet Michelle and her family. She introduced herself as Melissa and even invited Michelle out to have coffee with her. Every week, Melissa made sure she talked with Michelle, and they soon started to hang out together. They would meet for coffee or Melissa would go to Michelle's new home and bake pies or cheesecake together. Melissa is gifted at praying for people, so when Michelle would tell her about being lonely, Melissa would pray the most encouraging prayers over Michelle.

Michelle eventually made more friends in this church, but she is still very close friends with Melissa. Every church needs to have a person like Melissa to do what our verse for today suggests – practice hospitality. Sometimes it surprises people when I tell them that Melissa has Autism. I know her church is so thankful for the gifts that she brings, and so is Michelle!

Prayer: Thank you, Lord, for Melissa and the gifts you have given her. Help others to follow her example as we show hospitality to people in our lives. In Jesus' name, amen.

Body Building

Day 4
Tim and Alex

Bible Reading: Acts 27:1-3

Key Verse: "The next day we landed at Sidon; and Julius, in kindness to Paul, allowed him to go to his friends so they might provide for his needs." Acts 27:3

Devotional: Several times in Paul's life, he looked to his friends for care, safety, and comfort. Even though he was a prisoner, our verse for today says that he was allowed to "go to his friends so they might provide for his needs." That is such an important part of the gift of friendship. We look out for one another and lift each other up during times of celebration as well as times of difficulty. I'm guessing that Paul's friends were able to help him physically, perhaps giving him food, medical treatment, and clothing. I also believe they were there to speak to his heart and encourage him in a difficult time of life.

Tim and Alex are those kinds of friends. They have been buddies in school for the past seven years. Both friends have been through ups and downs of life, just like all of us. Through it all, they can count on one another for support, courage, and encouragement.

While there are so many Tim and Alex stories, I want to tell you about one of them. Tim is one of the most amazing young men I have ever met. His days are filled with many threats to his body, because his bones break very quickly and easily. This means he has spent a lot of time in hospitals, with doctors, and with other patients. One time, when his pastor had come to pray with him, Tim quickly requested that he stop at a child's room across the hall because that person was really sick and needed prayer. This heart of compassion is common to Tim, as he is quick to look to the needs of others around him.

I know, however, that there are times when Tim needs encouragement too. It's not easy to break a bone at the beginning of summer and know that plans for vacation and outdoor fun times will need to change. That's when Tim can always count on Alex. They can sit for hours and play video games, hanging out together and finding ways to turn lemons into lemonade. I think of Tim in the role of Paul – at the front lines of where God is working in those hospitals and spreading God's love. I think of Alex as Paul's friends, there to "provide for his needs" as life becomes difficult at times. I know that God has given them to one another as a gift, and I am thankful for how they can build one another up.

Prayer: People who have a disability can have both up and down times. There are some things that might be more difficult for that person. Perhaps someone gets sick more often or frequently feels upset or sad. How could you encourage that person? Is God asking you to be an "Alex" for someone? Ask God how He might use you in the life of someone who needs encouraging. By doing that, you allow that person to be a "Paul" and minister to others in return.

Day 5
Adam and the Football Team

Bible Reading: I Samuel 20:35-42

Key Verse: "Jonathan said to David, 'Go in peace, for we have sworn friendship with each other in the name of the Lord, saying, 'The Lord is witness between you and me, and between your descendants and my descendants forever.' Then David left, and Jonathan went back to the town." I Samuel 20:42

Devotional: Jonathan and David were great friends. They loved each other. They even told God about their friendship, committing to be close friends forever. Do you have someone in your life who is that kind of close friend? Jonathan and David enjoyed being with each other, and they also protected one another. They took this friendship very seriously.

I think that Adam is absolutely one of my favorite people. He is outgoing, checks up on his friends with his cell phone, cares about the events in the lives of his friends, and enjoys a good laugh. Many people recognize Adam as a great friend. He also happens to have Down Syndrome and Autism.

When Adam started high school, his size and love for sports made him a great candidate to help with the football team. The coach was very open to this idea. Adam joined the group and helped with equipment and making sure everyone had water when they were thirsty. He exercised with them, and he participated in the team values they all shared – everyone looks out for one another on this team!

One day at school, Adam was having a hard time in the hallway. Some of the other students didn't know or understand Adam, so they started making fun of him. That was not acceptable to the passing football team members. They made it crystal clear to the students that Adam was a member of the team, and would also be protected by his teammates. They took this friendship very seriously. In fact, they still do. Even though Adam and his football team have graduated from high school, he still gets calls from these friends to go out in the evenings. When Adam's mom died this year, his football friends spread the word and surrounded him at the funeral home. Several years later, they still take this friendship very seriously. Adam frequently calls them and finds out about their lives, and they include Adam in special events and outings.

I'm not sure what happened during football practice, but I wonder if they didn't say words similar to what Jonathan and David promised one another. Praise God for close friends who care, protect, and love each other.

Prayer: Have you ever committed to a friendship before God like David and Jonathan did? Is there someone in your community with a disability that you may want to befriend like the football team did with Adam? Consider talking to God about that friendship.

Body Building

Day 6
John and Ryan

Bible Reading: Romans 15:1-7
Key Verse: "Accept one another, then, just as Christ accepted you, in order to bring praise to God." Romans 15:7

Devotional: There are many ways we can praise God. We could sing, read a praise Psalm, tell a story about what God has done in our lives…or we could have a friendship like John and Ryan. Sometimes we don't think about friendship as a way to praise God, but our verse tells us that when we accept one another, we can bring praise to God. Perhaps there is a shout of praise in heaven when John and Ryan get together.

They have been friends for many years. When John and Ryan were in first grade, they would chase chickens around our yard with light sabers. When they got older, they would play video games and watch movies together. They have had sleepovers and playovers and know each other very well. Ryan is a loyal and forgiving friend. John is a great interpreter for Ryan because some people find him hard to understand. Ryan has Down Syndrome.

Some people over the years would go up to John and tell him what a nice boy he is to be so good to Ryan. Well, it's true. John is good to Ryan. The reverse, however, is also true. Someone should go up to Ryan and tell him what a nice boy he is to be so good to John. You see, John and Ryan have a mutual friendship. They enjoy being together and looking out for one another. Their puzzle pieces are firmly attached together, and each has benefited from the friendship.

When John got his driver's license, he picked up Ryan to go out to a movie. Ryan enjoys the fact that John can drive, because that is something that he isn't able to do. Ryan, however, contributes a great deal to John's safe driving. Every day since first grade, John has been on Ryan's "list." This is the list of people Ryan prays for each night before going to bed. Because Ryan is so consistent, he doesn't forget. John drives the car, and Ryan covers them in prayer. This is a God-designed friendship, and as John's mom I know that God uses this friendship to help form his amazing heart and character. Thank you, Ryan, for being my son's friend through the years, and please keep praying for him. May the time you spend together bring a shout of praise to God as you continue to accept one another.

Prayer: I want to challenge you to make heaven a noisier place. Think about how you can "accept one another" in such a way that brings praise to God. Ask God to show you some people in your life who might not feel accepted right now. Pray about that situation and ask God to guide you as you reach out to that person.

WEEK SIX

Day 7
Jonathan's Son and King David

Bible Reading: II Samuel 9:1-13
Key Verse: "…and Mephibosheth lived in Jerusalem, because he always ate at the king's table, and he was crippled in both feet." II Samuel 9:13

Devotional: When David and Jonathan formed their friendship before God, they talked about the relationship in terms of their descendents as well. Not only would this friendship impact David and Jonathan, it would also touch the lives of their children. Even after Jonathan's death, King David remembered this promise and followed through in a way that we can learn from today.

Even though most of King Saul's family, including Jonathan, had been killed, David wanted to show kindness to anyone from that family who might still be living, because of the friendship he had with Jonathan. As he was asking for information, he found out that "there is still a son of Jonathan; he is crippled in both feet." King David brought Mephibosheth to Jerusalem and honored him with riches in land, but he also gave him a place at the king's table. Our verse tells us that "Mephibosheth lived in Jerusalem, because he always ate at the king's table, and he was crippled in both feet."

The king's table was an important place of honor. Typically, the sons of the king would join him at that table. David honored his friendship with Jonathan by giving Mephibosheth the right to sit with the King.

I have heard stories from Christian schools and churches about people with disabilities being sent away and asked to leave. When this happens, I often think about the story of Mephibosheth. He earned the right to sit at the King's table because of whose child he was. We are given the right to sit at God's table because of whose child we are. As God extends His arms to each one of His children and welcomes them into His body, who are we to send someone away? After all, it's God's table, and the King has the right and authority to decide who sits in that place.

Other communities have discovered the joy of sitting at the table together. May God bring that kind of welcoming picture to your church or school as you form friendships that will last for an eternity.

Prayer: Lord, thank you for inviting us to your table. Without the gift and sacrifice of Jesus, there would be no opportunity to be with you. Help us to greet those around us at the table with the kind of love that brothers and sisters have for one another. In Jesus' name, amen.

Body Building

A Story of Your Own

Do you have a friendship with a person who has a disability? Tell us about that friendship. Remember, if you would like to do so, follow the instructions in the back of this book and send it to us. We want to learn from your stories. If it's OK with your friend, include a picture of the two of you together.

Introduction: Meet the two of us

Things we like to do together:

Ways I help my friend:

Ways my friend helps me:

Something our friendship teaches me about God or being a Christian:

Instructions for Submitting Stories and Photographs for "A Story of Your Own"

I look forward to learning from you. Please consider submitting your stories to CLC Network as you complete the activities under "A Story of Your Own." It is important, however, to always have permission from anyone included in your story before you send it to us. Here are the steps you should follow:

1. Write the "A Story of Your Own" story.
2. Make a copy of the permission form found in this book or download one from the CLC Network website at www.clcnetwork/BodyBuilding.
3. Share your story with the individual who is highlighted in the devotion.
4. If that person agrees to sending us the story, fill out the permission form and mail it along with a copy of your story to CLC Network, 4340 Burlingame Ave. SW, Wyoming, MI 49509 Attn: Body Building Story.
5. In addition to mailing the permission form, please send an electronic copy (and optional photograph) to glue@clcnetwork.org. In the subject line, please put the words "Body Building Story."

How CLC Network may share your story:

1. We will publish on our website (clcnetwork.org) some of the stories we receive. Check the website for frequent listings and updates. Remember, no story can be listed without the permission form.
2. *Body Building: Devotions to Celebrate Inclusive Community* is the first book in a series. The next book may feature some of the stories you submit.
3. CLC Network publishes a newsletter entitled "Inclusive." Look for some of the stories in that publication as well.
4. Many of the CLC Network consultants also speak at conferences and churches. We may share some of the stories as part of these meetings.

Body Building

Story and Photo Release Form

Send to: CLC Network
4340 Burlingame Ave. SW
Wyoming, MI 49509

Permission to use photograph and/or story

Individual's Name: _____

Contact Information for person submitting the story and/or picture (name, address, phone number, email address):

I grant to CLC Network, its representatives and employees the right to take or use photographs and story of me and my property in connection with the above-identified name. I authorize CLC Network, its assigns and transferees to copyright, use and publish the same in print and/or electronically.

I agree that CLC Network may use such photographs and/or story of me with or without my name and for any lawful purpose, including for example such purposes as publicity, illustration, advertising, and Web content.

I have read and understand the above:

Signature: _____

Printed name: _____

Organization Name (if applicable): _____

Address: _____

Date: _____

Signature, parent or guardian: _____

(if under age 18 or guardian assigned)

About the Author

Barbara Newman is a church and school consultant for CLC Network. She is the author of *Helping Kids Include Kids with Disabilities*, *The Easter Book*, *Autism and Your Church: Nurturing the Spiritual Growth of People with Autism Spectrum Disorders*, the *Church Welcome Story* and *School Welcome Story*, and *Any Questions? – A Guidebook for Inclusive Education*. She has written curriculum for Friendship Ministries, was a major contributing author of *Special Needs SMART Pages* for Joni & Friends, co-authored the *G.L.U.E. Training Manual*, and is a frequent national speaker at educational conferences and churches. In addition to writing and speaking, Barb enjoys working in her classroom at Zeeland Christian School. To contact Barb, call her at 616.748.6022 or email her at glue@clcnetwork.org.